Perfect PR

TO TRACEY, MICHAEL AND SOPHIE

Marketing Toolkits Series

Perfect PR

■ Iain Maitland

INTERNATIONAL THOMSON BUSINESS PRESS
I(T)P® An International Thomson Publishing Company

London ● Bonn ● Johannesburg ● Madrid ● Melbourne ● Mexico City ● New York ● Paris
Singapore ● Tokyo ● Toronto ● Albany, NY ● Belmont, CA ● Cincinnati, OH ● Detroit, MI

Perfect PR

Copyright © 1999 Iain Maitland

I(T)P® A division of International Thomson Publishing Inc.
The ITP logo is a trademark under licence

British Library Cataloguing-in-Publication Data
A catalogue record for this book is available from the British Library

First edition published 1999

Typeset by J&L Composition, Filey, North Yorkshire
Printed in the UK by Clays Ltd., St Ives plc

ISBN 1–86152–221–5

International Thomson Business Press
Berkshire House
168–173 High Holborn
London WC1V 7AA
UK

http://www.itbp.com

CONTENTS

Diskette

The diskette accompanying this title features 30 forms to help you plan and run your PR campaign. All the forms are set up as Microsoft Word 6.0 documents to allow you to customize each form to suit the needs of your company. All the documents can be opened through the File Manager in Windows. The document titles and respective page references are given below. Each document is saved in a separate file and they are labelled from tab01.doc to tab30.doc.

List of figures

Acknowledgements

I wish to thank the following organizations for providing information or assistance in the compilation of this book. Special thanks are due to those* that allowed me to reproduce their materials within the text.

Advertising Association
Alliance and Leicester plc*
Association of Conference Executives
Association of Independent Radio Companies Limited
Audit Bureau of Circulations Limited
British Association of Conference Towns
Bolton Institute
Capital Radio
Conferences and Exhibitions Diary
East Anglian Daily Times Company Limited
English Heritage*
Harrogate International Conference Centre*
Institute of Practitioners in Advertising
Institute of Public Relations
IPC Magazines Limited
Maclean Hunter Limited
Meetings Industry Association
Periodical Publishers Association
Public Relations Consultants Association
Radio Trent
Shepherds*
Suffolk Group Radio plc

Introduction

Perfect PR is written for you – the owner or manager of a prospective, new or existing business who intends to conduct a public relations campaign, perhaps for the first time. Here's what it includes:

- **Planning PR Activities**

  Chapter 1 shows you how to assess all aspects of your firm to ensure you have the information you need to make a success of a campaign. It goes on to look at the main PR tactics that you will employ – press releases, interviews and press conferences. It investigates the media too – the press, radio and television. And it highlights the importance of knowing your audiences and explains how to plan and schedule PR activities for the coming months.

- **Issuing Press Releases**

  Chapter 2 covers compiling a press list, deciding what to say in your press releases and details the nitty-gritty details of actually writing press releases yourself – paper, colour and typefaces, layout, contents and plain English, photographs, captions and other material; all the ingredients for success. It also outlines how to circulate press releases most effectively, handle responses and follow through to increase your chances of coverage within the media.

- **Managing Interviews**

  Chapter 3 sets out the main do's and don'ts of interviewing; whether with journalists, radio or television presenters. It considers the additional core skills that you need to succeed in press, radio and television interviews. As significant, it spells out the crisis management tactics that you should employ if the media come knocking on your door to ask about a faulty product or some other problem. And it tells you how to follow up interviews to ensure media coverage.

- **Organizing Press Conferences**
  Chapter 4 guides you carefully through planning a conference for the first time and choosing the right venue, speakers and invited audience. It details how to speak successfully in public and manage the press conference well. As important, it explains how to follow up the event to maximize your chances of further publicity in the media.

- **Running Your PR Campaign**
  Chapter 5 pulls together everything covered so far; and tells you how to assess a trial run and monitor responses to your initial PR activities. It explains how to bring in experts to assist you with your planning, and how to continue with your campaign and make a huge success of it.

The book is also packed full of action checklists and real examples of the key documents used in PR activities, plus the names and details of useful contacts, books, magazines and directories for further reading, and a helpful glossary of terms – all combining to make *Perfect PR* an essential, hands-on manual throughout each and every PR campaign, now and in the future.

1

Planning PR Activities

■   'PR' is – or certainly should be – a very simple activity. It involves putting across a positive message through suitable media to the right audience at an appropriate place and time; in order to establish and maintain a first-class relationship with your customers and any other people and organizations that come into contact with your firm. If they feel good about you and your products and services, they are more likely to do business with you! To make a success of planning PR activities, you need to look closely at:

■   your firm

■   PR tactics

■   the media

■   your audience

■   PR activities

Your firm

Start by analyzing your business; both internally and externally – you need a full and complete understanding of what's going on around you if you're to go on to publicize yourself successfully. Not least, you want to know what it is you should promote to the outside world; and what you want to keep to yourself! Look at the workings of your business, your products and services, your competitors and the marketplace and carry out additional research if necessary.

The business

Conduct a wide-ranging, in-depth assessment of your firm; taking account of its organization, structure and operations. Consider its location too. Is it well sited for customers, for example? Can it be accessed easily on foot and/or by car? If so, perhaps this is something that you'll want to publicize to your customer base. Think about its premises; size, facilities, image and so on. Visit each department in turn, talking to colleagues and employees about how the firm operates in practice. What aspects are worth publicizing – or not? You should find that this assessment will enable you to identify positive features that you weren't aware of; and can incorporate within your PR activities. Likewise, it should highlight negative features that should not be mentioned in your campaign; and that need to be resolved in the near future.

List your firm's strengths – as your customers see them. This is the information that you will want to put across in any PR activities. One small business trader – the owner of a tyre and exhaust fitting centre – sketched out notes which included the comments, 'My premises are spacious and roomy which enables me to set aside a waiting room for customers; with tea and coffee available for them to drink.' Another business person – a director of a mail order firm – put 'I employ a friendly and knowledgeable team who handle enquiries in an engaging manner; all complaints are dealt with on the spot, and followed up by the employee concerned to guarantee customer satisfaction.'

Make a note of your firm's shortcomings too; again from your customers' viewpoint. You'll want to work out how to remedy these – but until then, you'll almost certainly want to avoid drawing attention to them in any PR campaign. The owner of a computer centre drafted notes which incorporated this statement, 'As a small shopkeeper, I don't have the financial resources to buy in bulk, so I can't compete on price.' In 1997, she avoided referring to prices in any of her PR activities. You may find that completing *Assessing your firm: an action checklist* (Figure 1.1) is helpful here. Do it thoroughly – you'll find that these notes will prove invaluable to you later on when you launch your PR campaign.

Products and services

Examine whatever you offer (or are planning to offer) to your customers. You know your product or service range best, but it's probably a good idea to look at each item and activity with specific regard to their ages, varieties, quality, uses, safety, reliability, availability, packaging, prices, guarantees and after-sales service; as relevant in your circumstances. Your goods and services are of critical importance as they will probably be the central focus of most of your PR activities. They have to be first-rate – meeting customers' needs, doing the job properly, being readily available, well-priced and so forth. However impressive your PR may be, you will not be able to sell unwanted or sub-standard goods; or at least not more than once (and most businesses rely on repeat sales for long-term success).

Separate each product's characteristics into positive and negative features. The positive ones should form the basis of your PR activities. What is it about your products and services that make them so good? As an example, you may note down that your most popular product is sold in the largest number of versions in your trade or industry, so customers have the widest choice. As with your business appraisal, it is important that you see things from the customer's viewpoint, not your own. What else? Perhaps it has passed all UK and European safety standards and recommendations, so customers know they are buying something that is totally safe.

The negative ones need to be listed as well. What is it about each product and service that may dissuade customers from purchasing it? A common problem faced by many businesses at one time or another is that they are selling 'old' stock; typically, new models have been launched before the older versions have been cleared out. So – even though these versions are often

ACTION CHECKLIST

THE BUSINESS:	ASSESSED BY:	DATE:
ASSESSMENT CRITERIA	BUSINESS STRENGTHS	BUSINESS WEAKNESSES
ORGANIZATION		
STRUCTURE		
LOCATION		
PREMISES		
DEPARTMENTS		
EMPLOYEES		
POLICIES		
WORK METHODS		
OTHER		
OTHER		

Figure 1.1 Assessing your firm: an action checklist

ACTION CHECKLIST

APPRAISAL CRITERIA	POSITIVE FEATURES	NEGATIVE FEATURES
PRODUCTS AND SERVICES:	APPRAISED BY:	DATE:
AGE		
VARIETIES		
QUALITY		
USES		
SAFETY		
RELIABILITY		
AVAILABILITY		
PACKAGING		
PRICINGS		
GUARANTEES		
AFTER-SALES SERVICE		
OTHER		

Figure 1.2 Appraising your product range: an action checklist

just as good and have been replaced only with new patterns, colours or whatever – customers don't want them. Filling in *Appraising your product range: an action checklist* (Figure 1.2) may be beneficial at this point.

The competition

Do consider your rivals – this information can prove invaluable to you during your PR activities. View their businesses in the same way that you assessed your own – organization, structure, operations, location, premises and so on. Try to recognize their strengths and weaknesses so far as customers are concerned; and how you can use these to your advantage. As examples, you may not want to publicize your location if you know that a rival can offer easier access, and free parking. But if your premises are large and enable you to carry more stock than your competitors – and therefore provide greater choice for your mutual customers – you may want to promote this aspect of the business.

Similarly, appraise their goods and services in the same, detailed manner that you looked at your own range – age, varieties, quality, uses, safety, reliability, availability, packaging, prices, guarantees, after-sales service and so forth. Ideally, you will be able to identify weaknesses in their product and service range, and can use this to promote the relative strengths of your own goods. But be careful not to get involved in direct 'knocking' of your competitors though. You need to be absolutely sure of all of your facts to be able to do this without fear of legal reprisals. You also need to be better than them in all respects to avoid a PR backlash from that company. And remember the expression, 'all publicity is good publicity'. It's not actually true – but the implication that you don't want to attract attention to your rivals is a valid one. Don't do any PR for them!

Consider your competitors' marketing activities in particular; and more specifically, any advertising that they do in the media. Perhaps they advertise heavily in a certain publication; the trade paper, for example. You may find that it will be less receptive to your PR advances in due course. Money talks unfortunately – that paper is not going to risk losing valuable revenue by promoting your firm against one of its main advertisers. Many publications are as dependent on their advertising revenue for their continued existence as they are on sales income. Study your rivals' PR tactics too; they may be very good at publicizing themselves; and you can learn from their activities. *Evaluating your competitors: an action checklist* (Figure 1.3) is worth completing now.

ACTION CHECKLIST

THE COMPETITION:		EVALUATED BY:	DATE:
EVALUATION CRITERIA		MAIN STRENGTHS	MAIN WEAKNESSES
BUSINESS			
GOODS			
SERVICES			
MARKETING ACTIVITIES			
ADVERTISING ACTIVITIES			
PR TACTICS			
OTHER			
OTHER			

Figure 1.3 Evaluating your competitors: an action checklist

The marketplace

It is sensible to develop a broad and detailed understanding of the main features of your current marketplace; and for any that you may be planning to enter in the near future. Familiarize yourself with its size, turnover and the way in which it is structured and organized. Get to know and join the trade bodies, and understand their roles, responsibilities and functions. Be aware of the regulatory organizations and what they do; and adhere to their codes of practice. Think about the other participants in the trade or industry; manufacturers, wholesalers, retailers and the like, Consider how your business fits into the market, alongside these varied organizations and activities.

Look outside your market; identifying the numerous influences that can and do affect it for better or for worse. Contemplate the political and economic environment. As examples, will changing government policies have an impact? If so, how? What about inflation – does that have an effect? Think about society and demographic developments. Perhaps changing public attitudes may affect you in some ways; an ageing population in others. Consider technological advances. Without doubt, these will affect your business, products and services in some way, shape or form. Contemplate laws as well – are there any new European directives in the pipeline that will have an effect on your trade or industry? You will probably wish to fill in *Analysing your marketplace: an action checklist* (Figure 1.4, overleaf) at this time and add it to your accumulating notes. You will find them invaluable as you begin your PR activities in earnest.

Additional research

Most of the information that you want to obtain about yourself, your competitors and the marketplace in general will be known to you; or be easy to obtain via sales, financial and miscellaneous records, and formal and informal communication networks. But inevitably, there will be some gaps that leave you with unanswered questions and incomplete notes. To publicize yourself as effectively as you can, you need to fill in as many of these gaps as possible. So speak to everyone that you can within your firm; paying particular attention to those at grass roots level that talk to customers, suppliers and the like. Become a customer of your competitors – or ask a friend to go on their mailing list, or a relative to go into their store and report back to you.

There are numerous other sources of information as well. For example,

ACTION CHECKLIST

THE MARKETPLACE:	ANALYSED BY:	DATE:
ANALYSIS CRITERIA	POSITIVE FEATURES	NEGATIVE FEATURES
CURRENT MARKETS		
FUTURE MARKETS		
TRADE BODIES		
REGULATORY ORGANIZATIONS		
OTHER PARTICIPANTS		
OUR ROLE		
EXTERNAL INFLUENCES		
OTHER		
OTHER		
OTHER		

Figure 1.4 Analysing your marketplace: an action checklist

trade and professional associations are a key source of information on competitors, the market and general information. Most will publish surveys, reports and other data. If you're not sure who your trade body is, the *Directory of British Trade Associations* published by CBD Research is a guide to over 650 professional and trade associations in Britain. You should be able to read a copy of this in a larger library (refer to the Further Reading section on page 145 for more details). The government is another helpful source of a broad range of information including; census reports, trade statistics and social and economic trends. You can check its full list of publications by contacting the Central Statistical Office (see the Useful Contacts Section on page 142 for details).

Libraries stock various publications that can provide useful background information and data. In particular, *Kompass* lists British companies in various categories, *The Source Book* provides marketing information by industry and service sectors, and *Marketsearch* contains market research reports on a wide variety of markets. Bear in mind that some libraries will carry out-of-date editions; so you may need to shop around. Specialized business libraries are worth visiting too – the London Business School Library and the Science Reference Library are both useful sources in their own right. Again, refer to the Further Reading and Useful Contacts sections.

Some Chambers of Commerce stock local, national and specialist surveys, reports and statistics that may contain information of relevance to you. The quality and competence of Chambers will vary as they tend to be run by local enthusiasts rather than professionals; but they're worth checking out nonetheless. Local authorities are another helpful source of advice and information in many instances; especially those with small business development units (or those with similarly-titled sections). They're certainly worth a phone call or visit. See the Useful Contacts section for more details.

PR tactics

Next, you need to know about the PR tactics that will enable you to publicize your firm, goods and services through the media to the outside world. You'll normally employ three tactics – press releases, interviews and press conferences. Let's look briefly at the benefits and drawbacks of these now; they are then detailed more fully in Chapter 2 Issuing Press Releases, Chapter 3 Managing Interviews and Chapter 4 Organizing Press Conferences.

Press releases

The aim of a press release – indeed of all PR tactics – is to provide a positive message to the media that will be passed on to their audiences; which will hopefully be one and the same as your own target audience! In their favour, press releases enable you to decide on your precise message, to phrase it as you want, and to distribute it to selected media at minimal expense. However, they are surprisingly difficult to write well. At the very least, they need to contain news and/or information that will genuinely interest the ultimate audience and – as important – will appeal to the journalist (or whoever is receiving it) too. The ideal press release offers a ready-made news item or feature that requires minimal effort to use. It is worth noting at this point that press releases are sent not only to 'the press' (newspapers, magazines and the like) but to other media such as radio stations and television stations as well.

Interviews

You may conduct interviews as part of your PR activities; typically with journalists in the press, and radio and television presenters. Interviews almost guarantee that you're going to get your message across – the media wouldn't waste their time if they weren't going to run the interview in some way. (Whereas there is the distinct possibility that the majority of press releases will be thrown straight into the waste paper basket.) In live radio and television broadcasts, it is up to you what you say, and how you say it. The message is being put over exactly as you want it to be – direct to the listening and/or viewing audience. Nevertheless, there are drawbacks. With press interviews, the journalists will interpret what you say – and what goes into print may not be quite what you expected. The journalists might have their own agenda; at odds with your own. And radio and television presenters may not ask the questions that you want, and could even query your responses. And it is often live – which can be incredibly nerve-wracking, especially first-time around.

Press conferences

These events can be scheduled into a PR campaign – and are often hugely effective. Again, you control the message that is being put across; and can support it with product displays and examinations, informal interviews with key members of the company and press releases too. It is an opportunity to create strong working relationships with media contacts, and to provide what they and their audiences require. But – and it can be a big but – they can be time-consuming and complicated to set up and run. The popular image of press conferences is that they are convened almost instantly for a sudden, sensational announcement – and they can be; but they're rarely as impressive and as effective as those that are planned properly in advance. Also, they can be costly. You may run a press conference from your business premises; but if you are sited some way from the media, it won't encourage them to attend. You may prefer to hire a hotel, hall or conference centre near to appropriate press, radio and television stations in order to boost attendance. And that's when the bills start to add up.

The media

A dictionary definition of 'the media' might read 'an all-embracing term used to describe any medium that enables one party to transfer a message to other parties'. For PR planners, the definition could be 'those media that allow us to put over a favourable story and/or image to our customers and the outside world; and without charge'. This usually means newspapers, magazines, other publications, the radio and television. When deciding which types and specific media to use, you'll have three questions that need to be answered to your satisfaction:

First – will this medium be interested in running this story? For example, your sponsorship of a local under 11's football team may appeal to the smallest, local newspaper; but few other, larger media. Second – is the story going to be read, seen or heard by my customers? As an example, your participation in a daytime radio phone-in discussion may generate good publicity for your firm with those people who are at home during the day; but is of little practical help if you're targeting business managers at work. Third – will the message be put across in the way that I want? For example, if you are interviewed by a newspaper journalist, you are often dependent on their interpretation of your statements; and few will let you see their feature before going to press.

Newspapers

Papers can be grouped into various categories – national dailies (*The Sun*, *The Times*), national Sundays (*The People*, *News of the World*), regional dailies (*East Anglian Daily Times*, *Yorkshire Post*), regional Sundays (Avon's *Sunday Independent*), paid-for weeklies and bi-weeklies (*Burnley Express*, *The Cornishman*), free weeklies and bi-weeklies (*Bucks Advertiser*, *Trent Valley Journal*). Many newspapers – national, regional and even very local ones – publish several editions. As an example, the *Daily Express* prints three – for Scotland, Northern England and Southern England. This is worth investigating in due course because your original instinct may be to ignore one newspaper because it is a 'national' whereas its range of different editions might effectively make it a 'regional' to all intents and purposes; and of value in your regional PR campaign.

All newspapers adopt a different approach to news coverage and reporting – just contrast the relative approaches of the *Daily Mirror* with the *Daily Mail* and *The Sun* with the *Guardian* to confirm this! Local and regional papers tend to have a widespread and in-depth appeal across and into all sections; by age, sex, and so on. They are more likely to develop a close and almost personal relationship with local people – featuring stories and issues about dogs fouling the parks, cable companies damaging the pavements, and the like. Nationally, newspapers are more likely to be bought by certain groups with – to generalize greatly – professionals favouring *The Times*, workers buying *The Daily Star*, and so forth. Love-hate feelings tend to exist towards many national titles; *Mirror* readers usually dislike the *Mail's* political views, and vice versa. *Times* readers find the *Star's* populist language and attitude not to their liking.

Many so-called PR experts focus on the 'circulation' of a newspaper when deciding which titles to approach for publicity purposes; and, to a certain degree, this has some validity. 'Circulation' refers to the number of copies of each issue sold, delivered or handed out – and generally, the more potential readers the paper has, the better; the wider your PR message will go. Clearly, circulations vary enormously – *The Cornishman* sells around 20,000 copies per issue, the *East Anglian Daily Times* about 50,000 and the *News of the World* approximately 5,000,000. As a rule of thumb – and useful to know if you're a PR planner – Sunday papers tend to have larger circulations than their daily equivalents because people usually buy more than one newspaper on that day for leisurely reading.

But the 'pass-on' readership – the number of people who look at or read a copy of a publication – is as relevant too; and rarely taken into account, even by PR specialists. The pass-on readership is always higher than the circulation. A daily paper may be looked at by colleagues at lunchtime, a Sunday paper could be read by several family members and a weekly newspaper might be passed round the office or the home several times. It is estimated that the readership of a typical paper can be some three to six times higher than its circulation. It's worth noting that a low circulation paper such as the weekly freebie may in fact be read by more people than the paid-for daily newspaper with a higher circulation – simply because it's around for a longer period.

For the PR planner, newspapers offer various advantages – you can publicize your business and its activities to a broad, cross-section of a local population and/or to groups scattered across the whole country. Your PR message can be changed from one newspaper to another to test the respective effectiveness of different approaches; or to put across a revised message in a particular area. Assuming that your news or story is topical and/or of sufficient interest, you can generate publicity quickly, on a given day, and even on an ongoing basis.

There are some disadvantages though. Most PR stories are fairly mundane, so the paper will fit them in as and when it suits them; not you. And you're in the journalists' hands too – if they've misread your press release, or misunderstood your comments in an interview, key facts may be omitted or be incorrect. Newspapers have some inherent weaknesses – they're rarely read in detail, from cover to cover or for any length of time. Some of the freesheets are binned automatically without even being flicked through. Readers' moods will vary as well – hot and edgy on the train journey home, cool and relaxed whilst eating supper – so it's hard to predict how your piece will be absorbed even if it's seen at all. Papers have a short lifespan – they're usually thrown away at the end of the day. So if the publicity material isn't seen first time around, it probably never will be.

Magazines

One way of classifying magazines is to separate them into 'consumer' and 'business' titles; and then sub-divide them into more defined classifications. 'Consumer' magazines can be broken down into 'general consumer' titles (*Candis, The Listener, Time Out*) and 'consumer-specific' titles (*Practical Parenting, Slimming, Waterski International*). Business titles are usually associated with particular products and services (*Engineering Lasers, Frozen and Chilled Foods*), jobs (*Dairy Farmer, Dairy Beef Producer*) and trades and industries (*Retail Week, Sheet Metal Industries*). Like newspapers, some magazines print more than one edition to reflect the individual interests of their readers in different regions. Do check this out – as a simple example, there's no point in having an interview with you running in a northern edition if your customers only ever see the southern one.

A magazine's circulation is usually based on the number of copies of an issue sold over the counter, posted to subscribers, pushed through letterboxes, handed out to passers-by or sent free of charge to named individuals. (This is known as 'controlled circulation'). As a rule, business titles have a small but very well-defined circulation; ranging from 1,000 to 50,000 or more. *Sheet Metal Industries* is around 1,700 per issue; *Dairy Farmer and Dairy Beef Producers* is about 25,000. Consumer titles tend to have larger circulations; ranging from perhaps 50,000 to several hundred thousand or more. *Slimming* sells about 120,000 per issue; *Candis* about 520,000. Generally, the broader a magazine's interests, the higher its circulation. It is worth noting that a magazine's pass-on readership – whether a consumer or a business title – is usually around ten times its circulation figure. As examples, *Vogue*'s is 9.8; whilst *Film Review*'s is an impressive 18.6. The majority of magazines are retained at least until the next one is published a week, fortnight or month later. They may be re-read between four and six times by each person during this time.

General consumer magazines feature subjects of popular appeal and interest both sexes, all ages and social grades; albeit in varying proportions. Special interest topics appeal to those who share common hobbies, pursuits and other concerns; often regardless of their sex, age, or other characterisics. Business matters may attract individuals or groups from a sector of a certain trade or from across a whole range of industries. But it is important to bear in mind that each magazine approaches its respective subject matter in different ways – serious, humorous, quirky, outrageous – so that even those titles which appear to be aimed at the same audience may have (slightly) different readerships.

Magazine publicity offers various benefits for anyone planning a PR campaign. You can put across your message to clearly defined, small and compact or large and extensive groups of people who tend to be well informed and interested in the subject matter. Readers often view 'their' magazine as a trusted friend or adviser; and this can confer status and credibility on you and your activities. Magazines also tend to be read in a rather leisurely and relaxed way and are thus more likely to be read fully and at length; so the opportunities for your story to be seen are that much greater. Unlike most newspapers, colour is available in the majority of magazines so any photographs of you, your products or premises will have more impact and appeal. Magazines tend to stay around longer than papers too; often until the next month's issue – so your story may be returned to again and again.

Be aware of the drawbacks though. Many titles are published at fortnightly, monthly or even longer intervals; so your PR activities need to be planned carefully; well in advance. In some instances, copy needs to be submitted many weeks ahead of publication – which makes it difficult for you to be topical, or react quickly to changing circumstances. Given the lifespan of most magazines – a big advantage in many circumstances, remember – it is difficult to predict the exact day or even week when your feature may be seen. This makes it hard to judge what will be happening at that time; and how exactly readers will be feeling as they look at your material.

Other publications

'The press' is not comprised entirely of newspapers and magazines (although in most cases, these will play the central role in your PR campaign). It also consists of other, often obscure, publications such as in-house journals like *Barclays News* and *British Airways News* – a whole hotch-potch of assorted, complementary publications that can take the form of newspapers, magazines, newsletters or news-sheets. There are an estimated 20,000 house journals in the United Kingdom; with an overall circulation of around 20 million. As such, they are worthy of consideration.

A typical in-house publication will be written by the company's marketing staff who will have been briefed to promote news about the firm, its employees and its successes in the marketplace to the readership; usually the members of staff, and perhaps some customers and suppliers too. A number of enthusiasts within the company – would-be writers in various departments – may also make regular contributions. The publication will normally be sent out for printing – although with the increased usage of computer systems in the workplace, more and more are being printed in-house instead nowadays. Publication may be monthly; or bi-monthly in most cases.

Circulation is usually low; perhaps between a few hundred to a few thousand at most – but they may be read by individuals and organisations that are extremely interested in the specific subject. And they are normally kept for some time (at least a month and sometimes longer) and looked at often during that time. In their favour, these media usually have status and credibility in their field – which can rub off on those firms featuring in them. Your PR message can reach a tight, well-defined audience that tends to be receptive and interested. Knowing who your audience is makes it easier to appeal to them successfully.

Against them, many of these publications are rather obscure – you may need to research long and hard, contacting potentially relevant companies until you find one (or hopefully more) that are right for your PR activities. Also, it has to be said that some in-house publications are written, published and distributed in an erratic manner. Much depends on the company's approach and attitude to internal communications and the enthusiasm and skill of the writers involved. Many publications are badly designed, edited and printed; which will reflect badly on you. Some employees do not read them or do so sparingly; therefore missing your coverage. The bottom line is that these other publications are a mixed bag – consider them fully and cautiously; a good one may generate terrific publicity for your firm; but the bulk of them will simply constitute a waste of your time and energies.

Radio

The last decade has seen huge changes in the numbers and types of radio station existing in the United Kingdom; both at the BBC and in independent radio. The developments within independent radio have been most dramatic; mainly as a result of the deregulation by statute that removed innumerable restrictions and allowed more and more stations to be set up. In 1990 – when the industry was deregulated – there were 107 commercial radio stations in the United Kingdom. Now there are over 300; and 30 or so new ones are continuing to be established each year.

The radio industry has not only increased in size; but in shape too – evolving from a mainly local medium into a local, regional and national one. Local stations such as Invicta Radio in Kent continue to serve community needs, whilst national stations such as Classic FM, Talk Radio and Virgin meet national needs. Not surprisingly, these stations all have different styles; to match their listeners' needs. Local radio stations traditionally offer a mix of music, news, phone-ins, competitions, traffic and travel reports, weather and so on – to meet the requirements of their rural or urban audience. National radio stations may do too; although some are increasingly specialized, such as Talk Radio with its ongoing mix of news, talk, discussion and comment.

Audience numbers for radio stations vary substantially. In terms of total population reached, a local station such as Classic Trax in Belfast can be heard by up to 540,000 people; whereas Kiss FM in London covers

9,700,000. Most radio stations will provide independently audited figures of what's known as their 'reach'; or estimated weekly audience. As examples; Classic Trax reaches 32,000 (or six per cent of its target population; Kiss FM reaches 1,091,000 (or 11 per cent of its target population).

The types of people who listen to the radio differ significantly too. The long held belief that only 15 to 24 year olds tune in is no longer accurate; audiences are changing as rapidly as independent radio itself. Most stations supply independently verified figures dividing their audience in a variety of ways; usually by sex, age (5–14 years, 15–24 years, 25–34 years, 35–54 years, 55 years plus) and social class (A – upper middle class, B – middle class, C1 – upwardly mobile, C2 – lower middle class, D – working class, E – those people on the lowest levels of subsistence, such as pensioners and the unemployed). As a general rule, commercial radio now appeals to a broad, cross-section of the population. Southern FM on the south coast, for example, plays mainly classic hits; and its audience 'profile' – or make up – is 50 per cent male, 50 per cent female, 23 per cent 15–24 years, 57 per cent 25–54 years, 20 per cent 55 years plus, 53 per cent ABC1's, 47 per cent C2DE's.

Listening habits follow similar patterns. The typical household – so far as one exists – has three to four radios dotted around the home; but are tuned into just one or two favourite stations. The audience – in terms of quantity – peaks at breakfast time with all types of people listening in, and then falls away steadily during the day; as people go to work, do the shopping, or whatever. The stay-at-home audience – comprising largely of home-based workers, the unemployed and pensioners – is boosted at teatime as people return from work; and then falls away again into the evening. Perhaps surprisingly, weekend listening patterns follow a similar trend.

Radio offers numerous benefits. It is known as a trusted medium. It is considered to be a friend by many of its listeners and some of them form loyal attachments to its presenters. If you are interviewed by a popular local radio presenter, that trust will rub off on you. This is also a very immediate medium; it enables you to react promptly to events, going on air with an instant response. And it is a direct one too – you are being heard by your customers; and can address them personally, saying whatever it is that you want to say; and in the way that you want it to be said.

However, radio has various drawbacks as well. The key one is that it lacks any visual impact. You're wholly dependent on sound for your success. Say you really have got a terrific business and a great product but you've a boring voice and can't handle the tension of a live radio interview; the listener will be distinctly unimpressed; and will have a negative image of 'you' – and that means you personally, that business, that product; everything! Another disadvantage is that the radio often isn't listened to exclusively – it's a background noise which just happens to be on whilst people are cooking a meal, having a bath, or mowing the lawn. You're going to have to do something extra-special to capture and focus their attention on you. And that's difficult to do.

Television

Many PR planners concentrate their activities almost exclusively on newspapers, magazines and radio stations; and ignore television completely. In the past, this was understandable – there were limited opportunities for smaller, local and regional companies to obtain coverage on BBC1, BBC2, ITV and Channel 4. But the current growth and diversity of television is now opening up the medium more and more – Channel 5, satellite and cable stations and now, digital television with the availability of literally hundreds of stations, and thousands of programmes. And all of these may be potential targets for your PR campaign.

The advantages of featuring on a television programme – an interview, a discussion, a debate or whatever – are considerable. You can put across your message visually – your audience can see you (and perhaps your products), hear what you have to say, and watch a service being performed. This can have the most enormous impact; certainly far more than a disembodied voice on the radio. Also, with the increasing specialization of television stations and programmes, you can address yourself to a very specific niche audience – if you're a manufacturer of sci-fi memorabilia for example, you can promote yourself on the sci-fi channel at the current time and in due course will probably be able to target even more accurately; to 'Dr Who', fans, 'Star Trek' fans and so forth. (After all, Sky are currently planning to launch no less than 60 music channels via 'Music Choice Europe'; in collaboration with Sony and Warner Brothers.)

There are some disadvantages. The bigger and more prestigious television stations and programmes will probably remain as difficult to access as they always have been for small and regional companies. The total viewing audience for television is going to remain much the same, but will be divided up into smaller audiences per station and programme; a problem if you're targeting a broad mix of people rather than specialist groups. Satellite, cable and digital television are expensive; so a large proportion of the potential audience will not be signing up for some time. (At present, only around 25 per cent of UK homes have satellite or cable; and of 10 million households that have access to cable television, only two million are connected.) And, of course, performing on television requires skill and practice – if you look uncomfortable, speak in a hesitant manner and convey a negative impression in any way, this will reflect badly on your firm, goods and services.

Your audience

Moving on with your preparatory work, you should study your prospective and/or current customers; as these are the people and organizations that you will almost certainly be targeting with your PR activities. You need to know as much about them as possible; not least so that you can publicize your business, goods and services in the right way and through the most suitable media. For example, there is little point in sending a press release to the *Daily Sport* if your customers read *The Times*; or vice versa. And in an interview, you may use technical jargon and slang if your customers are fellow specialists; but will need to simplify your language if they are members of the general public. Here's the information you need to possess about your customers so that you can publicize yourself in the most effective manner.

Individual customers

Name; age; sex; personal status (young single adult, young married adult, married with children, etc.); employment status (part-time, full-time, self-employed, unemployed, retired, etc.); social grade (A: upper middle class, B: middle class, C1: upwardly mobile, C2: lower middle class, D: working class, E: those on lowest levels of subsistence); income bracket; credit status; address; type of address (terraced, semi-detached, detached, etc.); status (owned, rented from private landlord, etc.); area (rural, urban, etc.); communication methods (telephone, fax, e-mail, etc.); current and likely numbers. Have a mind's-eye view of your target customer, 'He's a young, single male living at home, with a high disposable income', for example.

Business customers

Name; type of firm (sole trader, partnership, private limited company, etc.); size (by turnover, number of employees, etc.); area of activity (retail, industrial, etc.); main products and services; main buyer (name, job title, department, contact numbers, etc.); address; region; communication methods (telephone, fax, telex, e-mail, etc.); present and likely numbers. Again, have an image of your 'typical' customer in your head – 'small shopkeeper, very price conscious, seeking value for money', as an example.

Habits

Type of account, orders, payments, balances, average order value, average payment time, average balance, credit limit; products and services purchased, when, how often and where; newspapers, magazines and other publications read, when, how often and for how long; radio and television programmes listened to and watched, when, how, how often and for how long; general opinions, likes and dislikes of your firm, goods and services, your rivals, their products and services, press, radio and television stations and programmes, presenters and contents.

As with the information you needed to obtain about your own business, products and services, competitors and the marketplace, much of what you want to know about your customers will be familiar to you – from your existing knowledge, databases, sales and financial records. Where gaps exist, the best advice is to talk to the people and businesses that matter – the customers themselves. Ask them what they read, listen to and watch; why; how, for how long and so forth. Of course, you may be targeting a new audience in an unfamiliar market; so some additional research may again be required; with trade and professional bodies, libraries, the government, chambers of commerce and so on needing to be contacted for advice and information. Refer to Further Reading and Useful Contacts sections. Completing *Identifying your audience: an action checklist* (Figure 1.5) may also be helpful to you at this stage.

PR activities

You're now ready to go on to plan your initial PR activities. To do this effectively, you need to decide on your message and tactics, and choose the

ACTION CHECKLIST

THE AUDIENCE:	IDENTIFIED BY:	DATE:
INDIVIDUAL CUSTOMERS	BUSINESS CUSTOMERS	CUSTOMER HABITS
NAME	NAME	ACCOUNTS DATA
AGE	TYPE OF FIRM	
SEX	SIZE	
PERSONAL STATUS	AREA OF ACTIVITY	PURCHASES DATA
EMPLOYMENT STATUS	PRODUCTS/SERVICES	
SOCIAL GRADE	MAIN BUYER	
INCOME BRACKET	ADDRESS	
ADDRESS DATA	REGION	MEDIA DATA
COMMUNICATION METHODS	COMMUNICATION METHODS	
CURRENT NUMBERS	PRESENT NUMBERS	OPINIONS, LIKES, DISLIKES
LIKELY NUMBERS	ANTICIPATED NUMBERS	
MIND'S EYE VIEW	MIND'S EYE IMAGE	

Figure 1.5 Identifying your audience: an action checklist

media that you'll approach to reach your target audience. You'll then be able to draft a provisional schedule to test your initial PR activities for the coming weeks and months.

Your PR message

You'll almost certainly have had a good idea of what your message to your customers was going to be before you started doing all this research into your business, products and services and so on. Typically, it will be something along the lines of 'Hey, listen – we're a great company. We've been around for ages and we're selling all the most popular models at rock-bottom prices!' That's what most business owners and managers want to say. But it's worth stopping for a few moments and thinking about this in a little more detail before you settle on this message.

First, you're actually putting across several messages here. 'We're a great company'. 'We've been around for ages'. 'We're selling all the most popular models'. 'We sell at rock-bottom prices'. Unfortunately, most of your audience will be confused by several messages at once. (Whisper this quietly – some of them are not that clever! If you want to confirm this, go and speak to those employees in your company that talk to customers, deal with their order forms and the like.)

Second, you're thinking a bit too much about yourself here. Let's take that initial message as an example – 'We're a great company'. Says who? You do? 'Well so what?' is your customers' response. Frankly your customers don't care; they're not interested in you or whether you're great or not. What they're interested in is themselves. And what they want to know is – 'what's in it for me? What am I going to get out of buying this firm's goods and services?'.

Third, it's always a good idea to ensure that what you say in your PR activities is true. Now it may well be the case that you do sell all of the most popular models and at the lowest prices – but it's worth checking to see that this is so. One thing you can be sure of is that customers will soon tell you if you're getting something wrong (usually just before they take their custom elsewhere) – and so too will your rivals; and perhaps others in the industry as well.

So, looking at what you're going to say again, let's settle on one over-riding message that stresses a really big benefit for your customers; and make sure it is true. How about 'Save Money at Gaythers – The Cheapest Store in Town'. That's your main message. As you progress with your PR activities, you may want to have other (related) messages at certain times. Perhaps there are occasions when you're introducing new lines and clearing out others; and you'll want to publicize these accordingly. But be consistent – if the over-riding message is 'save money!' then these other messages should reflect this.

Tactics

Decide on the PR tactics that you are going to employ – press releases distributed to media contacts in the press and at radio and television stations, interviews with journalists and presenters, and press conferences for media contacts to attend. In practice, you will probably try all of these approaches – at least in the early days as you're discovering what works and what doesn't work for you. Remember that your PR tactics are normally being addressed to the media rather than direct to the ultimate audience; your target customers. So don't just bear in mind that main 'save money' (or whatever) message for your customers; think about what the media want as well. Typically, a journalist wants a story that is presented in a near-perfect format; that can be re-written easily and with little effort for the next morning's edition. If you can satisfy that want – and interest your mutual audience as well – you're on the way to getting free publicity in the media.

The media

Make a note of all of the different types of media that may be worth approaching. Be completely non-discriminatory here; include everything that seems a possibility. That way, you aren't likely to miss out anything suitable! For example, if you're a small business operating in Suffolk, your list might include local newspapers, local radio stations and regional television stations. Below the various headings, you then need to discover and put down all the possible ones that exist within each category. As an example, your local newspapers would include the *Eastern Daily Press*, *East Anglian Daily Times*, and *Evening Star*; amongst others. You'll then need to add all the radio stations and television stations that are in that region; SGR FM, Anglia Television and so forth.

To draw up a complete list of newspapers, magazines, radio stations and television stations for any part (or all) of the country, refer to a publication known as *British Rate and Data* (BRAD). This is a 600-page directory that provides extensive, up-to-date data on the widest possible range of press, broadcast, electronic and outdoor media in the United Kingdom. Published by Maclean Hunter Limited, a copy should be available in larger public libraries; or you can purchase one direct from the publisher. See the Further Reading and Useful Contacts sections at the back of this book for further details.

Additional information about these media – and others such as newsletters and in-house publications – may be obtained from friends, colleagues and other professional contacts. Never under-estimate the importance of a personal recommendation or lead – as with most things in life, it's not what you know but who you know. An introduction by a friend to the editor of an appropriate in-house publication may prove to be absolutely invaluable in due course – if nothing else, it cuts out all the chasing that is normally required to establish contacts in the media. There is also a host of representative trade bodies in the press, radio and television industries that can supply valuable background details and advice; and often without charge. Refer to Useful Contacts again for names, addresses and telephone numbers.

Moving on, call each organization and ask for a 'media pack' – this is a brochure or booklet that sets out detailed information about the newspaper, magazine, radio station or television station. Most of the organizations on your list will publish one; and provide it free of charge on request. But note that they may call it by a different name – 'marketing guide', 'advertising pack', as examples. Refer to the Glossary of Terms at the back of this book for definitions, when necessary. Some publications simply supply what's known as a 'rate card' that lists advertising rates, audience figures and make-ups, copy deadlines, on-sale dates, the names and extension numbers of key employees, mechanical information and the terms and conditions of the acceptance of advertisements. Of course, these packs, guides, cards or whatever they're called are designed for prospective advertisers – but you'll find them informative too.

With newspapers and magazines, ask for a copy of the latest issue as well. Having these (and listening to and looking at potentially relevant radio and television programmes) will allow you to study and evaluate editorial and advertising content. This hands-on knowledge – when combined with the data in the information packs – will help you to decide which media may be worth targeting with PR activities; and how. As examples, the editorial content will give you some ideas of how your news and stories may be presented – will they enable you to put over your message in the right way? Similarly, the style and contents of the advertisement will offer some clues too – are they brash and upbeat, for example, or cool and factual? Does this reflect the message that you want to put across; and the way that you want to impart it?

Your audience

If you're going to put all your time and efforts into making a successful PR campaign, you'll want to make sure you're directing your energies towards those media that will allow you to reach your target audience. Too often, PR planners go by gut instinct. They personally like a particular paper or radio programme and assume that their customers will do as well – so they mark it down for PR approaches. It's better to do a proper analysis though – you'll be surprised at how often gut instincts are wildly inaccurate. To do an assessment, check through the various media packs and rate cards you've received, and make a careful note of the respective audience figures and their breakdowns for each medium. Next to these details, write out the key data about your customers – you'll have obtained this information from your earlier analysis (refer back to Figure 1.5 on page 25). Having all these facts and figures together in front of you will allow you to compare and contrast them properly. Completing *Comparing audiences: an action checklist* (Figure 1.6), on the following page, may be useful now.

Don't be taken in by the hype of how many people can potentially read, hear or see the medium. The fact that a radio station, for example, has a transmission area across six counties and may be heard by several million people is almost wholly irrelevant to you. However wide its transmission area and whoever has the opportunity to tune in, it does not mean that they will. 98 per cent of the population has a television set – so nearly 60 million people have the opportunity to watch an obscure television discussion programme going out at 3.30 am – but we all know that they won't. Ignore the sales hype.

Instead, look at the 'profile' of each medium's audience and compare it to that of your target audience. 'Profile' refers to the make up of an audience; typically, in terms of sex, age, social grade, and so on. Evidently, you initially want to retain those media that are read, listened to or watched by those people who match your customer profile most closely; deleting the rest. As a simple example, there is little point in targeting a mainly male audience if your customers are mostly women; nor young listeners when your ones tend to be older. Consider the 'penetration' of each medium too. 'Penetration' means the extent to which a medium

ACTION CHECKIST

MEDIA AUDIENCES:	COMPARED BY:	DATE:
MEDIA AUDIENCE	TARGET AUDIENCE	PROFILE/PENETRATION MATCH
NUMBERS	NUMBERS	
AGES	AGES	
SEXES	SEXES	
SOCIAL GRADES	SOCIAL GRADES	
LOCATIONS	LOCATIONS	
OTHER	OTHER	
OTHER	OTHER	
OTHER	OTHER	

Figure 1.6 Comparing audiences: an action checklist

reaches your target customer base. Again, you want to retain those media that are read, heard or seen by the largest possible proportion of your target audience. As an example, perhaps you are seeking to publicize your business to the estimated 100,000 15–24 year olds in an area; and one medium reaches 25,000 – 25 per cent of your audience; whereas another reaches 50,000, or 50 per cent. Clearly, the latter appears to offer better prospects.

Your PR schedule

Knowing what you have to say and how you will put it across to the media that will enable you to reach your target audience, you can draft a provisional schedule for your PR activities. This should set out: your message (typically the overall one; and others at different stages of your campaign); the PR tactics you wish to employ (press releases, interviews with the press, radio and television, press conferences); the media that you intend to target (perhaps the local press and radio stations) along with brief details (for example, name, profile and penetration figures, contact names and numbers). The type of information that you might record can be included in 'PR Schedule', shown as Figure 1.7. You will also need to add some data about the proposed timings of your activities and the costs involved.

Do think carefully about when you are going to carry out activities in order to generate publicity; perhaps during a particular week, month or quarter. Much will depend on your business, products and services – again, your earlier notes will be invaluable here. For example, if you're planning a new product launch in the spring, you'll want to pencil in some PR work just before and at around this time. Your plans may also be influenced by your competitors, the market and, of course, your customers. As an example, perhaps you've discovered that most consumer spending is carried out at the end of a certain quarter; so you might decide to conduct the bulk of your PR activities immediately prior to and at that time.

Consider the frequency of your PR activities. Again, much depends on the nature of your firm, goods and services, competitors, marketplace and customers. If you're constantly launching new and updated products or are selling goods that are purchased very often, you'll probably want to carry out more frequent promotional activities than if you weren't. Similarly, fashionable and/or seasonal goods and services that are popular for only a short period implies that more frequent publicity

PR SCHEDULE	COMPOSED BY:	DATE:							
WEEK COMMENCING									
DETAILS									
PR MESSAGE									
PR TACTICS									
TARGET MEDIA									
COSTS									

Figure 1.7 PR schedule

is needed, albeit for a limited time. Of some significance, if customers are moving in and out of the marketplace very rapidly, you'll probably have to promote yourself more often so that new customers are made aware of your business. This is where your notes will continue to pay dividends.

Think about the duration of your PR campaign too – which will once more be determined by the type of business, goods and services, rivals, market and customers involved. For example, short, quick-fire bursts of publicity may be appropriate if you are holding clearance sales regularly, are trying to sell seasonal goods or want to boost sales for a brief period of time. But ongoing, drip-drip-drip publicity may be better if you are happy with a steady turnover through the year. Only you can decide what's right in your individual circumstances.

Give some thought to the media too; and their schedules. The press have copy deadlines – and if material is not available on that date, it won't be included. Make sure press releases are sent in plenty of time – rate cards will provide details of deadlines. Likewise, radio and television programmes are planned in advance – so find out when is the best time to get in touch with them with your PR material. Think about the attitude of the media as well. As an example, if you distribute just one or two press releases each year, you've got a good chance of having them considered for publication. Why? Because they're different; the journalist doesn't see your press releases much. You must have something important to announce! But if you churn out releases every week, they may get tired of seeing the same material all the time.

One of the many perceived benefits of PR is that it is 'free' – unlike advertising, you do not have to pay for any publicity received in the press, on the radio or on the television. However, there are obviously going to be some costs involved – and you need to be aware of these, and to budget for them in this PR schedule. With press releases, there's at least the cost of paper, ink, faxing, e-mailing, postage and packaging to consider. For interviews, you might have to pay for the cost of a telephone call to a journalist, a journey to and from a radio or television station; and perhaps even some new clothes. To set up and run a press conference, you might have to hire a room in a hotel, provide refreshments and so on. And then there's the time you're putting into this PR campaign – this should be calculated and costed out as well.

Having settled on your timings and the costs involved, you can add this information to your PR schedule. You'll also find it is helpful to compose a publicity planner chart too. This is simply a ready reference chart that can be pinned up in a meeting room or wherever, to be checked

PUBLICITY PLANNER	CAMPAIGN:	COMPILED BY:	NUMBER:												
	DURATION:	SIGNATURE:	DATE:												
WEEK COMMENCING															
ACTIVITY															

Figure 1.8 Publicity planner chart

and amended as you go along. It enables everyone to know what's happening, when and where. An example is reproduced as Figure 1.8. And that's it – you're now ready to go on to launch your first batch of PR activities!

2

Issuing press releases

■   Press releases – one or two page summaries of positive news and/or information sent to target media with a view to obtaining publicity – will almost certainly play an integral role in your PR activities. For many DIY PR planners, these are the first point of contact with the media, and form the basis of features not only in the press, but on radio and television programmes as well. To encourage the media to either use them or to call you for further details or an interview, you need to know all about:

■   compiling your press list

■   deciding what to say

■   paper, colour and typefaces

■   structure, contents and plain English

■   photographs, captions and other material

■   circulating press releases

■   handling responses

■   following through

Compiling your press list

To begin with, you should compose a press list. This is simply a database of your contacts at relevant media – and will prove to be absolutely invaluable to you during a PR campaign. The information on your database should include; names, publications/stations, types of news and features covered, audience (profile and penetration) data, telephone (and extension) numbers, fax numbers, e-mail addresses, property addresses and postcodes. It is useful to have some sort of 'comments' section where you can record snippets of information that may come in helpful at some stage. For example, you could note how a journalist likes to receive information (perhaps by fax), when they prefer to be phoned (possibly at the beginning of their shift before they start writing), what hours they work, and so on. As another example, you may record that a journalist's partner is going into hospital for a minor operation; and could ask about this next time you speak. This might help to build a closer relationship with them. See Figure 2.1 for an example of a *Press contacts list* – you may want to use it or something similar as the basis of your database.

So how do you create and build this press list? We've already seen in Chapter 1 Planning PR Activities, that you can identify your target media by referring to *British Rate and Data* (BRAD); approaching them for media packs and rate cards; and subsequently using these to decide which newspapers, magazines, other publications, radio and television stations enable you to put across your PR message to your target audience in the right manner. The most effective way to compose your database is by simple hard graft – call each of the media in turn, and ask to speak to the most appropriate person. For most publications (except small and/or specialist newsletters, magazines and in-house productions), the editor will be too far removed from the day-to-day writing to be of value to you. You'll probably want to approach the news editor or features editor, or a particular journalist who writes regularly about your locality, trade or industry. For radio and television stations, you might want to contact a presenter – on local radio stations, for example, most presenters are

PRESS CONTACTS LIST

COMPILED BY: LAST UPDATE:

CONTACT / MEDIUM	PROFILE / PENETRATION	NEWS / FEATURES	TELEPHONE / EXTENSION	FAX / E-MAIL	ADDRESS / COMMENTS

Figure 2.1 Press contacts list

approachable; although on larger ones and television stations, you may need to go to their producer.

It is essential that you can build and maintain friendly relations with as many relevant people as you can – that is, those journalists, presenters and producers that work in your target publications, radio and television stations. Ask if you can come to see them; have a coffee or meet for a drink in their nearest pub. You'll find that many will agree; if there's a possible story in it for them. And you wouldn't be doing this if there weren't one, would you? Create a working relationship – your press releases, phone calls and so on are more likely to be read or accepted by someone who knows you than a person who does not. And if you're doing something for them – giving them an easy-to-write feature, an interesting news item to read out on air or whatever – you're halfway to getting the publicity that you want. As always, remember that the more you can do for them, the more likely they are to help you.

Deciding what to say

When you planned your PR activities, you will have decided what you wanted to achieve during the different stages of your campaign. Typically, your aim will be to publicize new and/or revised goods and services as and when they are being launched; in order to generate sales. Or perhaps you simply want to raise the overall profile of your business in the marketplace; making potential customers more aware of your activities and encouraging them to buy more products and services from you. So what message should you be putting across to journalists and their (and your) audiences to support these aims; and to help you to achieve them?

Don't write about the main features of your business, goods or services. Why? Because the chances are that these won't interest anyone at all. Journalists receive piles of press releases every day of the week – in the post, through fax machines and by e-mail. And most of them are mind-numbingly boring – because the company sending them has assumed that something of enormous interest to it will be equally interesting to the media, and their audiences. As an example, a company may have spent thousands and thousands of pounds conducting detailed, face-to-face interviews with a representative cross-section of its audience, and has produced masses of statistical evidence to show this, that and the other. Who cares? The journalists and their readers certainly don't. They aren't the slightest bit interested in the cost, the size of the sample, the interviewing methods used; nor the bar charts that highlight the findings. Yet this is what some companies put in their press releases. So what do they want? They wish to know what's in it for them!

Journalists want to read something that can be turned into a news story or feature for the next edition of the newspaper, magazine, or whatever. Now there are certain ingredients that will help you to sell a story to a journalist. That's not to say that if they're not included in the press release your story won't be covered – but their presence will certainly help. In general, the media prefer news to features; human interest stories rather than ones about businesses, products and services; anything involving children, animals and well-known people instead of middle-aged men in suits; stories supported by photographs (as long as they can be used); and perhaps surprisingly, good news rather than bad. (Not that you'll be promoting your shortcomings!) If your press release doesn't have such an angle, try to incorporate one in some way. As examples, a new product launch is 'news' on the day it goes on sale; a 'feature' at other times – so get your timing right. Put in a photo of the product – but not one showing a man demonstrating it; use a child. Why? Because it's so easy to operate, even a child can do it!'.

The audiences want to know about the benefits of buying from your business and/or using your goods and services. So don't tell them about the cost of that research, the interview methods and techniques or the statistics that you have acquired – just tell them how they're going to gain by purchasing products from your firm; and by using your services. This is a good time to look at all those notes you composed in Chapter 1. Does your business offer them free parking and/or easy access to the widest choice of goods, as examples? What about those products and services – are they the cheapest in the market, for example? Will you deliver and install items, and without charge? See yourself from the customer's viewpoint – decide what will make them buy from you; and then stress those selling points.

Paper, colour and typefaces

Once you've decided where the press releases are going to go and have some idea of the key message that's going in them, it's time to look at the nitty-gritty details – the paper you'll use for the releases, the colour of the paper and the text, and the typefaces of the text.

Paper

Most firms have their own printed stationery; letterheads, envelopes, compliment slips, invoices, credit notes, debit notes, statements, and so on. This is designed to convey a particular image of the firm – as a well-established and traditional business, as a modern hi-tech one, or whatever. And it should put across a unified image too – so the paper, colours and typefaces used should be the same; whether on a letterhead, a debit note – or a press release! So; use the same paper at all times. If you have not yet arranged stationery supplies for your business, the most appropriate paper for a press release is probably a lightweight, watermarked sheet with a matt finish. This tends to be the most popular kind used by PR companies; it looks classy and distinguished, enables black and coloured text to be read easily; and is relatively inexpensive. Visit your local stationers or out-of-town superstore to see what's available.

Colour

Similarly, the colour of the paper used in your everyday business correspondence should be used for your press releases too – again, to convey a consistent and professional impression to the outside world. If you are making your choice for the first time, white is the most popular selection for releases – not least because it enables text to be read easily. As an alternative, lighter shades of lemon, pink and grey put over a calm and professional image; and still allow text to be read without difficulty. Be wary of darker colours – they may create a very strong and powerful image of your business, but will cause problems for journalists trying to read from them. It is often most sensible to pick white paper, and then personalise it with a coloured logo, border and/or text. As an example, putting your company logo in the top right corner of the release makes it readily identifiable, having 'Press Release' in large red or blue letters is very eye-catching, and underlining key points in colour can be very effective too.

Typefaces

The size and shape of the letters of your text should reflect those used on a day-to-day basis in your business. If you have not yet decided what to choose, a simple typeface – Arial, Century Schoolbook, Times New Roman – is often the wisest choice. These look classy and are easy to read. More

Arial	Franklin Gothic Book
Bell MT	Garamond
Book Antiqua	Helvetica
Bookman Old Style	**Leawood Medium**
Century Schoolbook	Perpetua
Courier	**Rockwell**
Eras Demi ITC	Stone Serif
Eurostile	Times New Roman
Formata Italic	Verdana
COPPERPLATE GOTHIC	**Palatino Bold**

Figure 2.2 Choosing your typeface: an action checklist

complex typefaces can covey the impression that you're straining for effect; and, as significant, are difficult to read – especially if they've been faxed over onto shiny, thermal paper. A number of different typefaces are shown in *Choosing your typeface: an action checklist* (Figure 2.2); see which ones appeal most to you. But always remember the bottom line so far as press releases are concerned – keep it simple. More than anything else, your release needs to be read; so encourage the journalist to study it by using a readable typeface.

Layout, contents and plain English

As important as the paper, colour and typefaces are the layout and contents of the text. You also need to know the do's and don'ts of writing in plain English.

Layout

Press releases usually follow a set layout – it is sensible to adhere to this so that your releases appear as professional as those being circulated by PR agencies. And bear in mind that journalists will automatically look in certain places for the information they want – encourage them to read on and run a story by giving it to them where they expect to see it. They won't spend their time hunting for it; they've got better things to do. Here is a step-by-step guide to getting it right:

Put 'PRESS RELEASE' in capitals across the centre of the top of the page. As an alternative, put 'NEWS RELEASE' – this tends to have a greater impact as it implies a sense of urgency; and boosts its chances of being used straightaway. But think carefully. You'll find that journalists will check the date of a 'news release' more readily than they would for a 'press release'; and will be more inclined to drop it if it's a few days old. It will seem out-of-date. So use 'news release' for important, 'here-today-gone-tomorrow' news; and 'press release' for longer lasting, 'feature' information. More imaginative companies put 'PRESS RELEASE' or 'NEWS RELEASE' heading down the side of the page instead: and in big, bold coloured text – this can be quite an effective house style; and may be one you want to consider.

Below 'PRESS RELEASE' (or to the side if you've put it alongside the page) print 'Release Date: '; and then state it – '7 September 1998'. Or state 'Embargoed until. . . . .' and then the relevant date. You may want to put an embargo on the press release if you're about to launch a new product, for example, and would prefer one co-ordinated wave of publicity at around the same time, rather than in dribs and drabs over a longer period. Make this line a prominent one – the majority of journalists will respect an embargo; unless they're in a hurry to fill a space, and don't look too closely at the release date. Make certain they see it! Of course, if it is absolutely essential that the news isn't published before a certain date, hold back the releases until the right time – and fax or e-mail them over for greater impact.

Place the headline in the centre of the page. Keep this simple, and self explanatory. For example, 'Thomsett Launches New Pushchair'. If you can bring in a key benefit (for the customer); all the better. As an example 'Thomsett Launches New Pushchair – Free Basket and Raincover worth £20.99 for Every Customer'. Avoid technical facts and figures, word plays and puns and lengthy, complicated headlines – journalists don't want to have to think what the headline means; or what the release is about. Don't spend your time thinking of a really snappy headline that journalists can use in their newspaper or magazine – each journalist will think of their own; they will not run the risk of using yours and seeing the same headline appear in several other publications as well.

After this, set out the contents of the release. Use plenty of headings within the text; this helps to separate the press release into easy-to-read chunks, and serves to signpost areas of key interest to the reader. Make sure your text is double-spaced. This looks easy on the eye; and gives a

PRESS RELEASE

RELEASE DATE: _____

HEADLINE

HEADING: _____
_____
_____

HEADING: _____
_____
_____

- _____
- _____
- _____
- _____

HEADING: _____
_____
_____
_____
_____

MORE

Figure 2.3 Press release: an action checklist

COMPANY NAME

TITLE OF PRESS RELEASE

NUMBER OF PAGE

HEADING: _____
_____
_____

HEADING: _____
_____
_____

HEADING: _____
_____
_____

END

CONTACT DETAILS

_____
_____

Figure 2.3 Press release: an action checklist (continued)

journalistic feel to the release. Journalists normally produce double-spaced text so that it can be edited easily; something they may want to do with your press release. Use bullet-points to break up larger areas of text; and to emphasize important points.

Put 'more' at the centre of the bottom of the page if your press release is running over onto a second page. The ideal release is short; restricted to one page; or two at most. If you're thinking of running to three, take a close look at your material – and edit it down to two pages by removing unnecessary, and/or repetitive text. The longer the release, the less likely it is to be read. Three pages of thick, densely filled text are daunting; few journalists will want to study them – instead, they'll simply go to the shorter, one or two pagers on the pile.

Start a second page with your company's name, the title of the press release and the number of the page – just in case this second sheet becomes detached from the first one. It happens. Reduce further the chances of this occurring by stapling pages together; paper clips fall off easily! At the end of the text, type 'END' in the centre of the page just below it. Last of all, provide contact names, addresses, telephone and fax numbers and (if appropriate) e-mail addresses for follow-up queries. Add a final touch, by having generous margins at the top, sides and bottom – maybe two centimetres at the sides, three centimetres at the top and bottom. It all helps to convey the right, professional impression. Look at *Press release: action checklist* (Figure 2.3) on the previous page as an example of how a press release should be set out. You may want to use this as a framework for your own releases; or as a checklist.

Contents

Having caught the journalist's attention with your short and concise headline, move on to the opening paragraph. Include the main thrust of the press release here to hook the reader, and sell the story to them. What is your sales pitch? A new product or service, perhaps. Announce the key benefit for the readers; not the features that you like most about it. Say you've redesigned your best-selling bed-settee. The journalist's readers aren't the least bit interested in the new technical specifications – they just want to know that it's cheaper for them, easier to unfold or whatever. Make this initial paragraph as brief and as direct as you can. You've probably got no more than ten seconds of the journalist's time to persuade them to read on. Aim to produce a stand-alone paragraph, comprising around 50 words over two or three lines. Don't overload it with additional details.

The remaining paragraphs of the press release should fill in the supporting facts and information. The easiest and most effective way of doing this is to follow the journalists' old maxim for writing a good story – the 'who-what-when-where-why' sequence. You can either have this at the back of your mind as a checklist as you write each paragraph, or can even use these questions as the basis of your paragraphs. To set you thinking: Who is the main player in this story? (Is it someone that the press will want to feature; and that the audience will find interesting?) What is the story all about? (What's in it for the audience?) When is the story taking place? (Is it at the right time for the media –remember those copy deadlines.) Where is it taking place? (Will the media want to go there to cover the story?) Why is this good news for the audience? (Remember – what are those benefits?)

There are two further points to bear in mind when writing the main text of press releases. Avoid humour of any kind. It is notoriously risky. Something that strikes you as being amusing when you're writing your press release on a Friday night will almost inevitably be misunderstood by the stressed-out journalist trying to produce a 500 word piece on Monday morning for that evening's edition. Subtlety, nuances, word plays and the like invite misinterpretation – so play it straight. Whatever you put down will be taken at face value.

Also, don't be tempted to add lots of technical data at the end; as some first-time PR planners do. Most journalists aren't interested in the more specific details. (Those that are can get in touch, as appropriate.) Instead, include some ready-made quotes – from your MD, satisfied customers; anyone that can be quoted in a press story. A word to the wise though – don't ask your MD or favoured customers for a quote; they'll not say what you want them to say! Instead, write out a quote for them to approve. That way, you'll get exactly what you want for your press release.

Plain English

Your spelling, punctuation and grammar must be correct. If you'll be writing your material on computer, try to use a program that checks these for you as you type, and underlines errors in red and/or green as you go along. If not, show your copy to a colleague for their comments and suggestions. This is a sensible idea even if your spelling, punctuation and grammar are perfect – other people may come up with improvements for its contents, for example.

PRESS RELEASE

Issued 25 February 1998

NEW SOFTWARE PACKAGE TO HELP ADVISORS SELL PORTFOLIOS OF TEPS

A new software package from Shepherds (Endowments) Limited will help financial advisors recommend the kind of investments all their clients want – the type that allow them to sleep at nights.

The software, the first of its kind in the market, can be used as an educational tool for the advisor as well as a powerful sales tool. It includes a full presentation of both TEPs and the packaged plans offered by Shepherds. A quotation system allows advisors to provide clients with individually tailored examples of how the plan works, together with the potential benefits.

Shepherds' flexible range of TEP investment plans are unique to the market. An exciting investment opportunity, they eliminate many/all of the risks attached to buying one-off policies.

Director Mike Abraham explaines, 'TEPs are attractive to investors because they benefit from the long term earnings of a heavily equity backed investment and the smoothing from year to year. But they can present risks. If an investor buys one policy with one year of its life to run, they take a gamble on that life company not choosing that year to change their bonuses dramatically.'

In the main, investors don't lose out too heavily. But why take the risk? Shepherds reduces the risk over a longer investment horizon, on average ten years or more, by providing structured protfolios (TEP-plans) with a balance of policies and life offices.

The result is a TEP investment which provides solid, above average returns. The investment is made with a combination of investor capital and extra capital from an investment loan. This extra capital allows Shepherds to include more policies in the plan, so increasing

/more . . .

Shepherds (Endowments) Limited, Borough House, 78–80 Borough High Street,
London SE1 1LL
Telephone 0171 407 9700. Fax 0171 407 9600

Figure 2.4   A sample press release

the spread and the potential return, and means only one, simple payment up-front by the investor.

The software package explains the process in detail, taking the advisor from the basic endowment policies to sophisticated investment portfolios in a few easy steps. Included with the package are a clearly written guide for clients and examples of the simple documentation required.

Abraham concludes, 'TEPplans offer excellent benefits for everyone concerned, given the good investment proposition and the fact that Shepherds takes care of everything, from balancing the portfolio to ongoing administration. With this new software, we've made them even easier for advisors to sell.'

Copies of Shepherds' TEP software package are available by phoning the company on 0171 407 9700.

Ends

Note to Editors
High-resolution colour images of the attached screenshots, taken from the software, are available on request.

Shepherds
Shepherds (Endowments) Limited is the UK's leading exponent of the design and provision of tailored financial products using Traded Endowment Policies (TEPs).

The Trade Endowment Plan (TEPplan) range of products offered by Shepherds is unique to the market. Using sophisticated actuarial techniques, policies are packaged together in a portfolio to spread the risk of under performance which can effect individual policies bought from a list. The care taken to balance each fund provides stability and consistency to the investor. In addition, the investment is funded through a combination of investor capital and extra capital from an investment loan, allowing Shepherds to include more policies in the plan. This increases the spread and the potential return.

Press Enquiries
Nigel Pritchard, PPR. Tel: 01932 828771 Fax 01932 853448.
Mike Abraham, Shepherds. Tel: 0171 407 9700 Fax 0171 407 9600

Figure 2.4 A sample press release (continued)

ENGLISH HERITAGE

NEWS RELEASE

40/0298   February 25, 1998

ENGLISH HERITAGE MEMBERS GET MORE FOR MONEY IN 1998

There are even more great days out on offer in 1998 for those joining English Heritage, saving pounds on entry to hundreds of historic attractions and action-packed events.

Great value joining fees give a family of two adults and all children under 21 a year's free access to over 120 English Heritage properties for just £43. This adds up to big savings on standard admission charges and a year round treat for keen explorers of historic sites like world-famous Stonehenge, Queen Victoria's Osborne House, Kenilworth Castle and Hadrian's Wall.

Members also receive free admission to Charles Darwin's home, Down House in Kent, opening this Spring following an intensive programme of repair and restoration, and Brodsworth Hall and Gardens, the Victorian country house in South Yorkshire voted Britain's favourite historic property for 1997 in the prestigious NPI National Heritage Awards.

New English Heritage attractions include an exhibition at Dover Castle in Kent recreating the sights and sounds of a dramatic medieval siege using computerised presentations and three dimensional displays. Visitors will experience the feelings of a soldier defending the great fortress from French attack in 1216.

[MORE]

Figure 2.5   Another sample press release

-2-

Pendennis Castle in Cornwall opens up secret World War II military defences this year and launches new exhibitions bringing 500 years of the castle's history to life through interactive displays in a hands-on Discovery Centre.

Members also receive free entry to the majority of over 600 colourful events - taking place from Easter to October - ranging from historic battle re-enactments to period fairs and teddy bears' picnics.   There are also discounts for the acclaimed English Heritage programme of open air concerts.

On joining, members receive a free 224-page full colour guide to English Heritage historic properties and map.   A quarterly "Heritage Today" magazine keeps members posted on activities and conservation news.

Individual memberships are £25 for adults (or £40 for two), £15.50 for senior citizens (£26 for two), £16 for 16 to 20-year-olds and £11 for juniors up to 16.   Joint adult and senior citizen membership is £33 and single parent families pay £25.   Life memberships are also available.   Call 0171 973 3434 for more information.

[ENDS]

For further press information, please contact:

Jane Lawrence, Tel: 0171 353 8403

or English Heritage Public Relations, Tel: 0171 973 3294

Figure 2.5   Another sample press release (continued)

Just as important, you need to ensure that your press release is readable – no matter how accurate your spelling and so on may be, the text needs to be easy-to-absorb. Sound friendly – it creates a more positive impression, even on a cynical journalist. There are two main tactics you can employ here. Use 'you' and 'your' in the text. 'You'll save up to 15 per cent by ordering in this way' sounds better than 'A discount of 15 per cent is available on these orders'. Similarly, use 'we' as and when you can. Again, 'We're here to take your call 24 hours a day' conveys a friendlier image than 'A 24 hour call service is available for customers'. If you sound pleasant and approachable, the journalist is encouraged to call you; to find out more, to ask for an interview or help with a proposed feature.

Avoid slang and jargon – it causes confusion if the journalist is unfamiliar with the words and phrases used; and makes it less likely that they'll use the release. Remember, terms and expressions that are used in-house and/or in your trade or industry may mean little to outsiders; such as journalists on local papers, for example. Think about every word you are planning to use; and include it only if it will be understood by the reader. If not, either provide a definition or better still, replace it with an understandable one.

Use short words, sentences and phrases at all times – they encourage the journalist to read on. Short words should replace technical and specialist ones unless you are absolutely certain that the reader will understand them; a journalist on the trade body's newsletter would, as an example. Break longer sentences with lots of clauses into several shorter ones. They'll be easier to understand. Paragraphs in a press release should be no more than around 50 to 100 words at most – and the shorter the better. Long paragraphs – especially those with complicated words and meandering sentences – are very offputting. Journalists are busy people, skimming quickly through releases for potential stories; they won't waste their time on those that appear difficult to read. There are two examples of releases on the previous pages – one a 'press release', the other a 'news release' – as Figures 2.4 and 2.5. Look at them now to see how they have been produced in terms of layout, contents and plain English.

Photographs, captions and other material

The majority of press releases are sent on their own; as a stand-alone news story or feature. But some will be accompanied by photographs (captioned or uncaptioned) and other material such as samples. Here's what you need to know.

Photographs

Including a photograph with a press release can significantly improve the chances of publication in the press. A photo draws attention to a news report or feature in a publication, adds interest to the text and – as more cynical journalists might tell you – fills a space on an otherwise empty section of the page. But you need to give some thought to what types of photograph will encourage journalists to run a story in the next edition of the publication.

Find out what each journalist can use – a good reason for a phone call – and give it to them. Some publications don't use photographs at all; others only print in black and white or in colour; some will ask for prints; other will want transparencies ('trannies'). All publications have different needs. For example, many local newspapers will not carry any photographs submitted with press releases – they employ their own photographers who will come out and take the pictures that their journalists want to illustrate the piece. It's a waste of your time and money to forward photographs in such circumstances. The bottom line is to check in advance, include whatever they want – or as an alternative, indicate at the end of the press release (just before the contact details) that 'b/w and colour prints/transparencies of XYZ are available by calling . . .'. This is particularly sensible if you are operating on a limited budget – you don't want to spend unnecessary sums on photographs that will be going straight through the office shredder.

Be imaginative; when possible. (Again, think about what the press wants from you – study the publication and see what types of photograph are used; some may only use passport-style photographs!) In general, very few journalists will be inspired to use a studio-based shot of your new product or a photograph of a man in a suit receiving a certificate. These are so boring and predictable! Instead, give the photograph some life – have a photograph of someone using your product (preferably a person who looks like that 'mind's eye customer' we talked about earlier – see page 23.) Or have a photograph of someone performing the service you offer (again, preferably a smiling member of your staff who best represents the warm, friendly and professional image that you want to convey to the world.) Give the photo a twist; add something different so that it stands out and is more likely to be used.

Employ a professional photographer. This is a must – simply because there is a huge gulf between the quality of a photograph taken by a well-meaning amateur using a cheaper camera and the professional using first-class equipment and film. Amateur photographs look just that – amateurish.

They often contain fundamental flaws – red-eyes, subjects to the left or right of the central focus point, even objects appearing to project from various parts of the subject's body – and are rarely sharp enough to get into print. The best advice here is to commission a professional photographer to come in for a morning or afternoon – perhaps when another event such as an open day or press conference is being staged – and encourage them to photograph the buildings, products and services, people at work, customers, presentations and so on. You'll then have a bank of photographs to use in catalogues, brochures, annual reports, press releases and on other occasions. See the section in Chapter 5 (pages 130–136) on employing specialists for further information about photographers.

Captions

In a press release, a caption has one over-riding role – to readily identify any accompanying photographs. Let's be frank, many journalists are messy workers, sitting at desks that are piled high with papers, press releases, sticky labels and the like. The chances are that any photographs will become detached from their press releases so they have to be easy to identify again. The best way of achieving this is to simply write an explanatory caption – 'Johnson's new baby harness, 'Babi – Rida', available from 1 October. Call Mike Reynolds for details; 01394 021025' – on the back of the black and white or colour print. Or clip a printed note to the transparency, and put them together in a protective, plastic cover. This is all you need to do.

As with press release headlines, avoid wasting your time thinking up a clever caption; something humorous, containing puns, word plays, or whatever. Sensible journalists will never use them – they don't want to run the risk of seeing 'their' headline reproduced in numerous other publications. You'll have wasted your time and efforts. Also, they'll want to choose a caption that suits their publications' particular approach to news and features. Leave them to do this – after all, it's their job not yours.

Other material

In addition to your press release and any supporting photographs, you may want to include other useful material that may encourage journalists to feature your news or stories in some way. An information sheet can be a helpful inclusion. This might give some extra, background data about your

ALLIANCE LEICESTER

HOMEBUYERS' REPORT
ISSUE 2

The second issue of this report which looks at people's intentions to move in the next twelve months shows that homebuying intentions remain steady with **one in ten adults** intending to buy a home in 1998, either for the first time or as a move from their existing property. Potential homebuyers also reveal the reasons why they haven't moved sooner and what would motivate them to enter the market this year.

Alliance & Leicester's Director of Sales, Stephen Jones comments:

66 *Our survey shows that although the events of the last six months including several interest rate rises and higher prices have dented people's enthusiasm for homemoving slightly, demand for property has remained fairly constant. However, it is clear that homebuyers want stability in both prices and interest rates in order to realise the home-buying intentions expressed in this survey.* 99

MOVING MOTIVATORS

So what changes would potential homebuyers like to see before taking the plunge and entering the market this year?

We asked all adults which personal, economic and property market factors were most likely to encourage them to move home with a mortgage.

Personal/Family Factors

Not surprisingly, higher wages and improved job security were as important to homebuyers now as they were six months ago. However, fewer potential homebuyers were relying on an inheritance or **windfall** to get them moving, mentioned by only 23% compared to 33% in last summer's survey when many people were eagerly awaiting their windfall shares from building society and insurance company demutualisations.

Property Market Factors

House price inflation was a factor close to the hearts of many existing and potential homebuyers. One in five said **lower property prices** would encourage them to move. Only 3% said they would like to see prices rise further, presumably to increase the value of their existing property.

Economic Factors

By far the most commonly mentioned factor which would encourage people to move sooner was **lower or steady interest rates**, mentioned by over two thirds of those surveyed, compared to just over half back in the summer. This change is undoubtedly linked to the fact that there have been four interest rate rises since our last research.

LABOUR AND THE HOUSING MARKET

Homebuyers were also asked how last year's change of Government had affected their attitudes towards home-ownership. This question was first asked directly after the General Election and six months on, over two thirds of adults are still saying that there has been no change in their attitudes under the Labour Government. Only 10% say they feel less positive under Labour – one in five of these citing interest rate rises as the main cause of this negative attitude. There has, however, been a slight change of heart in London and the South East where immediately after the election, 16% of homeowners in London and the South East said they actually felt more positive about the housing market with Labour in power. Six months on, this figure has halved to just 8%.

Figure 2.6 A sample information sheet

FIRST TIME BUYERS OUTNUMBER MOVERS

Of those one in ten adults intending to buy in the next twelve months, first time buyers represent a slightly higher proportion than next time buyers. There is also some evidence that there may be a shortage of properties for first time buyers as potential next time buyers delay putting their properties on the market. Of those next time buyers who intend to move this year, less than a quarter have got around to putting their homes up for sale, whereas 30% of first time buyers are already actively looking for a home to buy.

Of those properties already **FOR SALE**, many had only recently come onto the market.

HOW LONG HAS YOUR HOME BEEN ON THE MARKET?

Less than 3 months	42%	
3-6 months	13%	
6-12 months	22%	
More than 12 months	18%	

WOULD MOVE, CAN'T MOVE

One in four existing homeowners said they would like to have moved sooner. Some regions have more 'frustrated movers' than others.

% Homeowners by region who would like to have moved sooner.

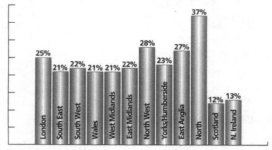

There are a variety of personal and market factors which have delayed people moving. The relative importance of these has changed in the past six months. Affordability was still an important issue but less so than in the summer with fewer people worried by job insecurity. In some regions, finding a property to buy has become more difficult, in others, homeowners have had difficulty selling their homes.

WHAT HAS STOPPED PEOPLE MOVING?

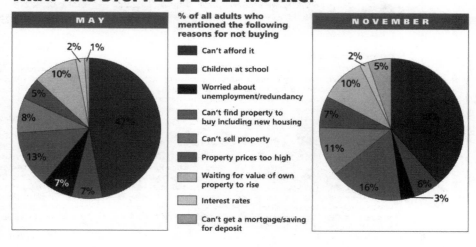

Figure 2.6 A sample information sheet (continued)

HOW MUCH DO HOMEBUYERS EXPECT TO PAY?

Our report showed that first time buyers' expectations of how much they will have to pay have risen considerably in the last six months from a national average of £51,000 to £57,000. Those who already own a property will be looking at an average price of £92,000 up from £73,000 in May.

Region	First Time Buyers	Next Time Buyers
SCOTLAND	£37,000	£83,000
NORTH	£33,000	£67,000
NORTH WEST	£41,000	£63,000
YORKS/HUMBERSIDE	£51,000	£82,000
WALES	£39,000	£58,000
W. MIDLANDS	£55,000	£82,000
E. MIDLANDS	£44,000	£58,000
EAST ANGLIA	£50,000	£88,000
SOUTH WEST	£48,000	£109,000
SOUTH EAST	£69,000	£109,000
LONDON	£78,000	£132,000
NATIONAL AVERAGE	£57,000	£92,000

NB – Northern Ireland figures are not shown due to insufficient sample size of homebuyers intending to buy in the next 12 months.

WHAT TYPE OF PROPERTY ARE PEOPLE LOOKING FOR?

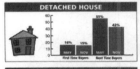

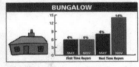
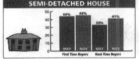

Significantly more first time buyers are now looking for flats than six months ago and far fewer next time buyers are expecting to 'trade-up' to a detached property. This may be a reflection of widespread price increases last year.

HOMEBUYING PROCESS

In the light of the Government's review of the homebuying process and in particular, the possibility of introducing anti-gazumping* measures, we asked homebuyers whether they felt an offer on a property should be legally binding.

The survey has revealed very strong feelings on this matter among existing and potential homebuyers. There was overwhelming support for this proposal among existing mortgage holders – with 85% agreeing with this statement. Recent 'first-time' movers who bought and sold in 1997 appeared to feel most strongly with 91% agreeing that an offer should be binding.

*Gazumping is where a seller accepts an offer for a property and then accepts a higher bid from another buyer. This practice becomes more prevalent in an environment where house prices are rising.

MORTGAGE PAYMENT PROTECTION

Our survey shows that there is some confusion among homebuyers as to how they would maintain their mortgage repayments if they lost their income through illness or redundancy. One third of existing mortgage holders said that they would claim on mortgage payment protection insurance. However, around the same number would try to set up mortgage payment protection if such a misfortune occurred.

Approximately one in six people said that a period of lost income would force them to sell their home and just as many people did not know what they would do. 17% said that they had savings to fall back on but 14% said that they would rely on state benefits, perhaps ignorant of the fact that for mortgages taken out after October 1995, there is a nine month waiting period for this benefit. Even then, only around half of the interest and none of the capital on the mortgage is repaid.

Figure 2.6   A sample information sheet (continued)

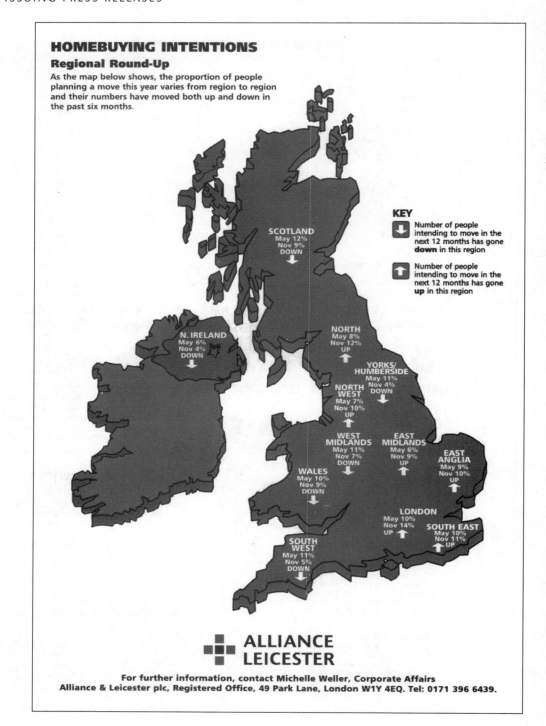

Figure 2.6 A sample information sheet (continued)

business, products and services, key personnel and the like. You can include those technical facts and figures here if you want! It can provide one or two ideas for a journalist who is looking to add a few lines to a piece which is perhaps 50 words short of the required length; and may also generate ideas for longer features or interviews with members of staff. An example of an information sheet is shown as Figure 2.6 – you'll find it follows many of the do's and don'ts of writing press releases.

It is tempting to include samples of your products, as and when appropriate. Typically, you might put in cakes and biscuits, pattern swatches, books, videos, CD-Roms – in fact, just about anything that you're selling as long as it can be posted (or hand-delivered) safely and without damage. Samples can grab the attention ('what's in that funny shaped package?'), interest the journalist ('mmm, that looks good'), and persuade them to read the press release ('what's this about?'). But it's arguable whether a sample actually boosts your chances of publicity very much. Journalists are bombarded with freebies every day; some they'll take for their own personal use; the rest will be handed out to other people or binned. To the journalist, the biscuit is eaten with a cup of tea; the pattern swatch is used as a coaster. The press release is all-important – it's that which gives them their hastily written filler half an hour before the deadline – not the eye-catching freebie that comes with it.

Bear this in mind – and the cost too. If you're giving away all these free gifts – 95 per cent of which will end up in the waste paper basket – you'll need to budget for their cost and any additional packaging and postage charges as well. It's more sensible to include a line in the press release to the effect that 'Review items are available on request, by calling . . .'. That way, you'll reduce the costs as only the more genuinely interested journalists will contact you for samples; hopefully those who will run a product review in their newspaper or magazine. But be careful though – more popular and expensive items will attract calls from journalists who want them for their personal use; regardless of whether they'll publicize them or not. It is sensible to ask for copies of their publication and for details of their planned features before releasing goods. Chase up copy to ensure you received the agreed publicity. Make it clear beforehand that you'll collect review items so that they can be used for review purposes again. And collect them!

You'll find that many publications – and some radio and television stations too – will be interested in the possibility of running competitions with your goods and services as prizes. This can work out well for both parties. The paper, for example, knows that competitions are always popular with readers and, if they can extend it over several editions ('collect six vouchers to enter the draw'), this will help to pull in readers. For the company, you'll get guaranteed publicity. But you need to set this against the cost of the prizes that you've provided. In short, will the competition generate enough sales to cover – or hopefully exceed that outlay? Often, it's a matter of 'suck it and see' when you start your PR activities. You won't be able to appraise their value until some time after the campaign – refer to Chapter 5 for assessment details. Only then will you be able to decide which competitions work and in which media; and can make changes for the future.

In general, competitions seem to be most effective if you are targeting members of the public – the response rate can be as high as five per cent, depending on the readership. (Compare this to the average one and half per cent response to direct mail shots, and it is quite impressive.) Be wary of offering competitions to business customers though – the response rate is often less than one per cent. Executives with company credit cards will not waste their time entering – if it's something they want, they'll simply charge it to the company. The only items that may appeal to them will be those goods that can't be put through as a legitimate business expense.

One idea that will work in your favour is to offer one outright prize plus numerous money-off vouchers. That way, you'll need to budget for the cost of the main giveaway; but the runners-up will need to come in to buy something from you. The money-off voucher may in effect cost you your profit on the sale; but they'll be paying for the basic cost of it. And you'll have got customers into your store – some old, others new – and they may buy more products and services; now and in the future.

After a while, you may find it useful to start producing 'press packs' for your main media contacts; those that give you publicity on a regular basis. A press pack simply contains a mass of ready reference material in a clearly labelled file or folder (in the company's colours; with a logo etc.). Typically, you'll include a copy of your most recent press release. Make sure this is reasonably up-to-date; say within the last month. Put in an information sheet too. This should focus on your main selling points; the very best bits of all-purpose information that you'd love to see featured in the media. Put some ready-made quotes in here. Finally, include some captioned photographs as well. Basically, you're providing a set of back-up notes and supporting information that journalists can turn to as and when necessary.

Circulating press releases

It is worth spending a few moments thinking about the different ways of forwarding press releases to journalists, presenters and producers at your target media; and to decide which is (or are) most appropriate for you in your situation.

Most press releases go by post. This tends to be a convenient and fairly inexpensive method; and can be the most suitable when the release is accompanied by photographs and other materials. However, they're usually sent inside manila C4 or C5 envelopes, and by second-class post – so they arrive looking nondescript, in a bundle of post, a few days later. This is hardly inspiring; it's just another humdrum press release to be added to the pile; it may or may not be used. And if the journalist has received a mass of post that day, they might not even bother to read it at all. It's junk mail – to be consigned to the wastepaper-basket straightaway.

If you decide to send press releases by post, try to make them attractive and appealing to the recipient. This is a great news story or feature you're offering to the media – you don't want it to slink in shame-faced, but to stand out from the crowd! Put it in one of the firm's proper envelopes; whether white, yellow, grey or whatever. Stamp the company logo in the top left or centre of the front of the envelope. Address it to someone in particular – 'Tony Hollis', for example – rather than the nameless 'Editor' or (worse) '*The Evening Star* Newsdesk'. Get the name, job title and address details correct – spelling names incorrectly can cause offence. And put a first-class stamp on it. Why? Because it's a first-class story!

You can send press releases by fax. These will have some impact; and create a sense of urgency and importance. They're more likely to be noticed, and read promptly. You may find this is the best method of sending news releases to daily papers, for example. But bear in mind that photographs and other supporting material will need to be sent under separate cover by post – and in a busy newsroom, they may not meet up with the faxed release a day or two later. Also bear in mind that faxing numerous press releases through to your target media is time-consuming.

If you're faxing a press release through, send it with one of your company's fax cover sheets – again to a named person, and make sure spellings and other details are correct. It is worth checking the number of the fax machine nearest to the journalist before you start faxing a press release. Larger organisations will have several and you don't want to fax something to the main fax machine by the switchboard if the journalist is working on the next floor and won't receive it until later in the day. Best of all, phone the journalist, tell them you've a fax to send to them – and ask for the number. They'll then go and fetch it.

Press releases can also be e-mailed. This creates a professional, cutting edge image of your business, is relatively speedy, and allows you to send scanned photographs at the same time. You'll be surprised at the number of times you'll be asked for a photograph by a journalist who needs it that very day. Often, the only way to supply this there and then is to e-mail it. Investing in a scanner and Internet access can be a good investment.

If you're going to e-mail, it is sensible to announce this fact in advance. Some journalists will only check their mail at the start and at the end of the day; and this delay in reading your material can prove costly; particularly if it's been sent to a daily publication. And of course, e-mail is still not yet available on a universal basis. So what should you do? The bottom line is to find out how each journalist likes to receive material – and provide it in that form.

Handling responses

You must be prepared to handle a potentially large and unpredictable response to your press releases – if successful, you are probably going to be phoned, faxed or e-mailed for more information, additional comments or an interview at various, unexpected times. You need to be available; and be able to give the answers and respond to requests straightaway – the journalist's deadline may be just hours off if they're working on a daily newspaper. Alternatively, other, well-informed members of the team need to be around to provide assistance. This may seem to be an obvious point when it is stated in this way – but it is surprising how many DIY PR planners aren't there when the journalist calls; and how few of their colleagues can help. 'I'm sorry, Mr Barham's away from the office until next Tuesday – and he's the (only) person who deals with all of our publicity' is a familiar refrain to journalists contacting companies for a quote or a transparency. The outcome? The journalist – or more likely numerous journalists – go elsewhere; to the big pile of other press releases on their desk.

So what should you do? First things first, you probably don't know how many approaches you will get; and there aren't any meaningful statistics to quote for press releases – so you'll need to make an educated guess. If you were sending unsolicited mailshots to prospective customers, you'd expect a response of maybe one to one and a half per cent (according to research); a mailing campaign to a well-targeted, interested audience might generate a response of possibly two to three per cent (according to trade figures); if you're sending press releases to carefully chosen, hand-picked journalists with whom you have established a good working relationship, you might expect a response rate of up to perhaps 10 per cent (as a rough and ready rule of thumb). Work to this figure until you've been issuing press releases for a while; and then you'll get to know that so-and-so always responds, someone else does occasionally, and another person never does. (This, of course, will also help you to target your press releases more accurately – but more of this later in Chapter 5.

Likewise, you don't know when journalists are going to contact you – but you can be certain that they won't be getting in touch when it suits you. If you work a 9 to 5 day from Mondays to Fridays, be ready to receive calls, faxes and e-mails at 7.30 in the morning and at 10 o'clock at night (the journalist may be writing a last minute filler to go into the next morning's edition). Also be prepared to receive them at weekends; even on Sundays. The biggest mistake that DIY PR planners make is to assume that the media work the same hours as they do and will only contact them at those times. The fact is that some will; others won't – and maybe it will be the journalist who calls you on a Sunday morning that will give you the biggest PR story of all.

You'll want to think about how journalists will respond to your posted, faxed or e-mailed press release. The vast majority will phone you – they want clarification of a particular point, a ready-made quote for a related article they're writing or a black and white print to illustrate a piece. A phone call is the easiest way of getting whatever they want; now! Some will want to fax or e-mail you a proposed article for you to check its accuracy and/or to approve it; and may ask you to fax or e-mail additional text or a photograph to them. Again, you need to be prepared for these common requests – and be able to meet them if you want to get that publicity.

So, how do you handle these responses? Here are the key guidelines; most of them are based on common sense – and yet so many PR planners fail to follow them. Don't do it all yourself – make sure that other people around you are involved and can deal with queries too; especially during your absence. Ensure that copies of the press release and supporting documentation are readily available to them. Give out-of-hours phone, fax and e-mail details on press releases – and for at least two people; you and a partner, for example. Ensure that phones and fax machines are plugged in and e-mail messages are checked regularly. Have relevant

ACTION CHECKLIST

PRESS RELEASES: **MONITORED BY:**   **DATE:**

PRESS RELEASE	SENT TO	DATE/METHOD	MEDIA RESPONSE	MEDIA COVERAGE	BENEFITS
TITLE					
MAIN MESSAGE					
KEY CONTENTS					

Figure 2.7 Monitoring press releases: an action checklist

information to hand at home. The bottom line for handling responses is to be available, be informed and be responsive.

Following through

You need to keep a careful record of your activities involving press releases, in particular; their main message and contents; to whom they were sent, where they were sent, how and when they were sent; the responses to them, by whom, how and when the responses were received; plus details of any coverage in the press or on the radio or television – dates, places, size or length of coverage, immediate and subsequent benefits (related orders, sales etc.) You'll find it useful at this stage to refer to *Monitoring press releases: an action checklist* (Figure 2.7) – you should be able to start filling in some of the left-sided columns now; and the rest as your PR activities progress.

Retain copies of all of your press releases on file (either by date or subject, as preferred), along with a note of the details of their circulation; to whom, where and so on. Ask any journalist you speak with to send you a copy of any features; some will do, which is helpful, others won't remember (or bother) – but this gives you a good reason to call them up at a later date to ask for a faxed copy; and perhaps 'sell' another story to them for the next issue. Don't forget to keep a record of these responses; by whom, how and so forth. And make a note to call journalists a week or two after the anticipated publication date if you have not received a copy of the paper or magazine.

Get someone from within your organisation to go through the other publications (and listen and watch any radio and television stations) that you have been targeting – it is not uncommon for your press releases to generate coverage without anyone telling you about it. (You will want to check these punctually so that you can be prepared for any feedback from the audience; and especially carefully to ensure that any information given is correct – you'll be surprised at how many stories contain inaccuracies, and need following up to be corrected.) This monitoring job is an ideal one for an office junior; as long as they can be relied upon to go through each publication conscientiously. Of course, buying all of the targeted publications can be expensive – and needs to be budgeted for if they are purchased exclusively for this purpose – but it has numerous, related benefits. As examples, it enables you to identify the types of news and features in the publications and keep up-to-date about what's happening in the market, which of your competitors are advertising, and so on.

Cut out and keep any clippings that are found; and make a note of the coverage in your action checklist. After a period of time, you'll start to build up a clearer idea of which newspapers, magazines and other publications are interested in which types of story – and you can then start to focus your PR activities with greater accuracy. Similarly, keep a record of any direct developments resulting from publicity in the media – customer enquiries, orders, sales and so forth. This will enable you to assess your PR campaign; and make changes and developments for the future. See Chapter 5 for more on assessing your PR activities.

3

Managing interviews

■ Your press releases and other regular approaches to media contacts on your list should generate interviews with the press and on radio and even television programmes too; thus enabling you to put your message across to your target audience, and in the way that you want. There may also be occasions when the media will approach you for interviews; perhaps asking for your opinion on industry changes and developments or, as often, about something negative – redundancies at your firm, a faulty product that you have sold, or a service that you have provided. So to manage all types of interview successfully – and to put across a positive, upbeat image at all times – you should know about:

■ Interviewing do's and don'ts

■ Press interviews

■ Radio interviews

■ Television interviews

■ Crisis management tactics

■ Following up interviews

Interviewing do's and don'ts

Too many PR planners are nervous of interviews – 'Will I say the right thing to the journalist?', 'Will my voice sound okay on the radio?', 'Will I look all right on the television?' – and view them as a negative experience. They worry more about themselves and how they will come across and less about the value of these PR activities – 'Am I going to come over as a wise expert?', 'Will I make a fool of myself?' are other typical questions. But an interview is the best thing that can happen to your PR campaign; it is a key activity of unlimited value. Here's why; and how you can make the most of each and every one.

The interview

First things first. An interview – whether in the press or on radio or television – is a great opportunity; an absolutely terrific chance for you to put your message across to the people who matter. And you are getting free publicity that would cost you hundreds or even thousands of pounds if you had to pay for it as advertising. And this interview is even better than advertising; it is in a magazine that readers trust or on a radio programme or a television programme that people enjoy; so they are already favourably disposed towards you. And they're actively reading, listening or watching – unlike advertising material in the press which is skimmed over to get to an interesting story, on the radio which is an opportunity to re-tune to another, music playing station or on the television which is a chance to put the kettle on or pop to the loo. So, the interview offers innumerable benefits for you, your firm and your goods and services. Grab the opportunity with both hands.

You

Let's get another thing straight about an interview – and those natural, first-timer's nerves and uncertainty that you might be experiencing about it. You are the expert, not the interviewer; nor the audience. You! This is your company and your products and services, your competitors, your market and your customers. You did all that research – see Chapter 1 – and know more about the subject than anyone else. So there is no question that can be raised that you can't answer; and no comment that you cannot expand and explain. You have nothing to be worried about. You can't be caught out. If anything, the interviewer should be worried about you – you have the knowledge and expertise to run rings around them.

The interviewer

In most instances, your interviewer knows relatively little about the subject – that's why they're asking you the expert. You may be being interviewed by a 17-year-old cub reporter on the local paper, the radio presenter who has just played the latest Oasis release and said happy birthday to six-year-old Lucy, or a television presenter who has skimmed through a page of scribbled notes about the subject, as prepared by a researcher, who's just looked at a book or report on the subject. That's not to mock them at all – they do what they do extremely well – but simply to emphasize the main point that you are the expert not them; so you have no need to be nervous. Surprisingly, you will also find that the interviewer is usually on your side, particularly on radio or television. The interview and the show in which it is taking place are there to inform and entertain the audience. So the interviewer wants you to be able to talk fluently, to answer questions competently; and to make the interview an enjoyable experience for the interviewer, you and the audience. You're a partnership whilst you're on air.

Your preparation

Preparation is the key to success in all interviews. That old 'who-what-when-where-why' sequence provides a useful framework here. Who is the interviewer? Find out about them before the interview – read their newspaper features, listen to their radio shows or watch their television programmes. Get to know them and work out their approach, whether factual, light-hearted, cynical, or whatever; and make sure that this suits the message you want to put across. Who else is taking part; in a radio or television discussion, for example? Discover their likely viewpoints, the points they might raise, and your responses to them. Who is the audience? Be sure that this audience and your target audience are matched closely; you'll have assessed this already if the medium is on your contacts list (refer to page 29 onwards) but should do it again if you've been approached by other, different media. You may not want to put significant amounts of time and effort into interviews that are not going to be read, heard or seen by your target audience. (But bear in mind that practice is always helpful; especially for radio and television interviews.)

What is the subject? You'll know what this is going to be, and will want to refresh your memory of the main points by re-reading all of those accumulated notes; or at least the action checklists that you completed (see pages 7, 8, 10, 12, and 25 in particular). What questions will be raised by the interviewer? Don't go and ask them; they're not going to tell you! Instead, put yourself in the place of that 'mind'seye customer' we talked about (on page 23) and calculate the types of questions that they'd raise. Then prepare the points that you want to put across (and remember, 'benefits' not 'features'). Don't plan answers too carefully though – you'll never be asked questions exactly as you imagined them, nor will the interviewer let you work through a lengthy, over-rehearsed sales pitch. Jot down a few key points on a postcard, and use this as a crib sheet as long as it will not distract you.

When is the interview taking place? If it is part of your schedule, you'll have plenty of time to prepare. But if you are being approached for an instant quote or reaction, the interview is now! So you need to be ready to answer questions there and then. This is where all that preliminary research – which may have seemed tedious at times – comes into play; you have a ready reference file and checklists to refer to. Make sure they're close to hand. How long will it last? Radio and television interviews will run for a set, carefully planned time so check in advance how long you're going to get so that you can plan accordingly. If you're getting one minute on the radio to talk about your newly designed computer program, you'll want to ensure that you get your main message across (its versatility, for example), but if you have longer, you can talk about some of the other benefits too (easy to install, simple to use, etc.).

Where is the interview being conducted? Press interviews may take place face-to-face (on your premises, at a pub, etc.) or, as often, over the telephone. Surprisingly, telephone interviews can be easier – you can record the conversation if you like (useful if this is a contentious issue), can refer to a checklist of points without embarrassment, and are less likely to be drawn into reckless, off-the-record comments. But – and an important but – you don't know if everything is being noted down accurately, so you'll need to check this, or provide a follow-up fact sheet confirming the main points. Radio and even some television interviews can be held over the phone too (much less stressful for first-timers), outside (make sure the view of your property is a favourable one) or in the studio (which gives the greatest potential for your voice and appearance to have an impact on the audience). If studio-based, ask to be shown around in advance to get a feel for the place.

Why is the interview taking place? You'll think you know the reason – because the media want to tell everybody about your great new product, or whatever. Wrong! The journalist may be trying to fill a space in their newspaper at the last minute, or the presenter might be attempting to make a show lively and interesting. Work out what the motive is; and help them to fulfil it; whether this means giving the journalist a quick quote, or suggesting a product demonstration on the programme. Finally, find out whether a radio or television interview is live or recorded. A live interview is often best – you have the chance to make your comments without interference or later editing, but it can be nerve-wracking. (Although you'll often find that this 'edge' gets the adrenalin pumping to produce a better performance.) A recorded interview seems less stressful; but it can make your approach sloppier as you know that it can be re-recorded. And – as significant – the interview can be edited. And you will find that edited comments may be taken out of context, and do not put across the full message, nor in the way that you want it to be put over.

Listening to questions

One of the two core skills of a successful interviewee is to always listen to what is being said. It's natural to dwell on the last question; and what you should have said in response to it ('. . . if only I'd mentioned the company name . . .'). And it's equally easy to worry about the next question; and what would be the best response ('. . . what if she asks me how it's actually been made, what will I say? . . .'). But it's too late to change the last answer; and you don't know what the next question will be! So it is far better to concentrate on the here and now, so that you can understand the meaning of this question and what's wanted, formulate what you should say and can then put across your key message; the benefits for the audience, and so on. In a press interview, you can get away with hesitation and uncertainty, and asking the interviewer to repeat the question because no-one else is around to form an impression of you; but on a radio or television programme, it will reflect badly on you, making you appear incompetent. You must be absolutely focused on one question and one answer at a time; hear it and be able to answer it.

Answering questions

The other core skill is being able to answer each question well – and this means a brief and direct answer that includes the main message and/or a benefit as and when possible. As important, speak in simple, clear English so that you know that the message is getting across, and being understood by the media contact and the audience. Simple words, phrases and sentences are easy to say – you're far less likely to stumble over 'and' and 'but' than 'in addition to', 'however', 'nevertheless' and 'notwith-standing', as examples. And everyone understands them – the person in the street, the specialist; everybody! But if you talk in trade jargon and use specialized expressions, you'll almost certainly confuse or alienate someone out there. You'll find that if you listen to programmes in advance of your appearance some radio and television interviewees start to 'talk posh'; and to put on a performance. You'll often hear their voices change, stiffen, and become more formal – and they sound tense and ill at ease as a result of it. Instead, speak naturally, and your confidence will be boosted, you'll feel good about the interview, and will perform more effectively.

Press interviews

Of course, these basic interviewing do's and don'ts are applicable to all interviews, whether press, radio or television. But each medium also has its own characteristics that need to be taken into account by PR planners and interviewees. The main feature of the press that is worth thinking about is that they control the message that you want to put over to the audience – when it is published, how the facts are put across, and where the feature is placed; front page, middle pages or wherever. Obviously, your main concern is to ensure that (so far as possible) the right message is put over; and in the best possible way. With this in mind, here are five key steps to follow for press interviews:

Work to deadlines

Do remember that the press work to deadlines – journalists' copy needs to be submitted by a certain date (or time for daily publications); and if it is not ready, it doesn't get published. So if a journalist calls for an interview, and you're unavailable (and no-one else can deal with it equally well), make sure that everyone knows that the message taken should include a note of the journalist's name, contact number (at various times), subject matter, and that all-important copy deadline. And return their call! Respect the deadline and work to it – if an interview has to be conducted, facts and figures need to be faxed or e-mailed or a photograph must be sent to arrive by a certain date, do it in time. If not, your competitor may be approached and quoted instead, other people's statistics will be used or your product will be mentioned, but without an accompanying photograph. In the press, the deadline rules – adhere to it, or lose out.

Record interviews

You may want to consider tape recording interviews with the press. The reason is a simple one – some journalists will misquote you; either unintentionally or deliberately, if they want to jiggle your words to fit a particular angle. In most instances, this is relatively insignificant – the fact that the MD's name is 'Jon' and not 'John', that the first version of a product was launched in '1993' and not '1992' and so forth are unlikely to do much harm, if any, to your PR message. (And certainly far less than the ill-will that might be created between you and the journalist if you pick up on each and every minor point, and try to correct it.) But you will want to ensure that you are quoted correctly especially if you are discussing a contentious issue; a tape recording of a telephone interview is one way of doing this, providing fact sheets and asking to see proofs are other, less pointed ways of monitoring the outcome of face-to-face interviews.

Avoid off-the-record comments

Don't make the mistake of telling a journalist anything 'off-the-record' or 'in confidence' on the basis that it won't be used; some journalists will respect it, others won't – and will mention the fact somewhere in the story. (They may attribute it to 'a company spokesperson', 'an industry source' or whatever, but they'll still use it.) And why not – if someone's daft enough to say it, and it gives the story the sensational headline, or a new angle? Also, don't make the mistake of thinking – as some first-time interviewees do – that anything said after the journalist's notebook is put away won't be used. It will be if it is relevant and adds a twist to the story. So – the bottom line is – don't say anything that you don't want to be used.

Provide a fact sheet

The best piece of advice that can be given regarding press interviews – particularly local press interviews – is to forward a thank-you letter, fax or e-mail saying how much you enjoyed and/or appreciated the interview, and repeating key facts and quotes from the interview. You will be surprised at how often inaccuracies creep into news stories and features; typically, the interviewer misheard a comment and wrote it down incorrectly, or misread their notes when typing it into their computer; or perhaps they relayed the story over the phone, it was written down, passed to another journalist, and so on. Your communication is an insurance policy; it boosts the chances of accurate facts being given, the 'right' quotes being used and so forth.

Ask for proofs

A few publications – mainly trade magazines – will give you the opportunity to see 'proofs' of the relevant article before the publication is printed and distributed. 'Proofs' are simply copies of the finalized versions of printed pages and are produced in order that they can be checked for errors, and last-minute changes can be made. Always ask if you can see proofs (so that you can check that facts are correct, quotes are accurate, and so forth). Your success here depends on the individual relationships you have struck up with journalists, how the approach is made (nobody wants to feel they're being checked up on) and the time involved – although with the increasing use of fax machines and e-mail, this should be less of an issue than it once was. If you are given the chance to look at proofs, keep your suggestions to a bare minimum and focus exclusively on changing incorrect (and therefore potentially damaging) statements relating to your firm, goods and services, rather than suggestions on style, approach and other contents. Most journalists will welcome the opportunity to correct inaccuracies, but are unlikely to respond favourably to other suggestions, however well intentioned.

Radio interviews

Like the press (and indeed, television), the radio has its own set of characteristics that need to be taken into consideration by PR planners. The key characteristic of the radio is that you can only be heard by your audience. This is a one-dimensional medium that is wholly dependent on sound; and you must concentrate on what you say and how you say it in order to succeed. Do follow the do's and don'ts of interviewing success in radio interviews described below.

Arriving at the studio

Arrive in good time. If you can listen to the radio station on the way in, you may find this helpful – it will give you a feel for what's going on, and whether they're trailing your interview or not. Don't have anything to drink prior to the interview; alcohol will take the edge off your reactions, and anything else will prey on your mind. First time interviewees always need to nip to the loo before the interview; if you're hesitating, go. That feeling will only get worse when you're on air. A key point – and perhaps a surprising one – is to dress for the interview, even though you can't be seen. Wear something that conveys the image you want to put across, and make certain that it feels comfortable too. You will find that this helps to get you into the part of a company spokesperson, and to create the right mood. It gives you confidence – try it, you'll see it works.

Your voice

Of course, your voice is of crucial importance in a radio interview; it's what the listeners hear, and they'll judge you (and your company, goods and services) as much on that as they will on what you say. So what should you do? Smile! It lights up your voice, adds colour and feeling and makes the whole interview sparkle. People will want to listen; you're a nice, friendly person, not a miserable so-and-so. Give your voice life as well – don't answer questions as if you're reading out a shopping list. You're having a chat with a colleague, a gossip with a neighbour or are telling a joke at the pub. Vary your pace; slow up to emphasize a point, speed up to get to the next key point, and so on. Adjust the tone of your voice too. Lift it and lower it as you talk so that it seems interesting, and listeners will be encouraged to turn up the sound.

Ending the interview

Try to end the interview on a high note; a summary of your main message, and the key benefits of shopping with your company, buying this new product, or whatever. You'll usually find that the radio presenter will give you this opportunity as the interview draws to a close – remember, they're on your side! But just as important, remember that this is their show though; they will have the last word, not you. So don't try to slip in an extra comment at the end; or a joke (and as a general rule, steer clear of humour in this and all interviews – something that seems funny to one person is meaningless or even offensive to another). Even if you succeed, you won't endear yourself to that presenter, and you do want to be invited back again, don't you? So the ending should simply be something like, 'Peter Walker, thank you for coming in.' . . . 'It's been my pleasure, Nigel.' Then wait for the radio presenter to finish off, and play that jingle.

Television interviews

Again, with television interviews, you should follow the basic do's and don'ts for interviewing success. But – like the press and the radio – the television has its own particular characteristics, and you need to take account of these in your interviewing techniques. The overriding characteristic is that you can be seen and heard; in colour and on a big screen, and in stereo sound! Every sigh, raised eyebrow and twitch will register with the audience. So you need to think specifically about your arrival, your clothes and body language, the camera and the end of the interview.

Your arrival

Arrive in plenty of time; as you would for any other interview or meeting. If possible, do a trial run the day before – and leave half an hour earlier on the day itself. Arriving early gives you a chance to check the running order of the programme, your part in it, and how you are going to be introduced – make sure it is an accurate description and that you're happy with it.

(You don't want any inaccuracies to go out on air; nor do you want to have to correct the interviewer – it gets the interview off to an edgy start, wastes time and can make you seem pernickety.) Also, check how your name and description will be superimposed on screen (if appropriate); again ensure that these are correct. (An obvious point perhaps, but often overlooked; and always on that one occasion when the company name is misspelt!)

You'll find that some interviewers will want to meet you beforehand; to get to know a little about you and talk through the interview; they might even want to rehearse. Others won't come near you – typically, because they want to keep the interview fresh and lively. And some others will be too busy; or self-important to mix with members of the public. The idea of a rehearsal may appeal to you – it's a chance to practise, run through the questions, and rehearse the answers. But it does tend to kill the subsequent interview stone cold dead – it removes all of its spontaneity, questions and answers become stilted and sound rehearsed (and there's nothing more offputting than that). And if the interviewer departs from the expected course, the interviewee may be thrown completely; particularly if they are inexperienced at television interviewing.

Clothes

Think about what you're going to wear – what will best convey the impression that you want to put across; whether professional, informal, approachable or whatever? For a professional image, you'll probably want to wear a suit, or something equivalent to this. To put over an approachable image, you'll usually prefer smart but casual clothes. It is also sensible to wear something that is lightweight – it can be hot in a studio, and heavier clothes will make you sweat (which makes you appear tense and shifty) and may stain easily (which looks unpleasant and ugly.) Make sure clothes are comfortable as well – this is not the time or place to break in a new (and itchy) shirt or stylish (but tight) jacket. Give some thought to the show you're going on – its backgrounds, style and what the presenters wear. Whatever it is that you're planning to wear should not look out of place.

As significant, you'll need to wear television-friendly clothes; jackets, jumpers, shirts, blouses, ties etc. As general rules, avoid stripes, checks, and lots of black and/or white; these tend to flare and blur on screen. Blue is usually a no-no as well; a popular television technique involves 'colour separation overlay' whereby the camera films against a blue backdrop, and another picture is then fed in as a backdrop from another camera. If you are wearing a blue top, whatever backdrop is being fed in will show up on that top. You should keep everything simple too; especially around your face and neck. Avoid tinted glasses, large earrings, and colourful ties; these all distract the viewer from your eyes and mouth, and what you are saying. (Clear glasses are okay though – the lighting will be arranged to avoid any glare and reflections. Never take them off – this will simply make you look bewildered during the interview.) Don't worry too much about make-up – this will be taken care of by the studio as well. Men in particular must – absolutely must – be prepared to have some applied; bald heads, foreheads and noses in particular can appear shiny and distracting without it.

Body language

Your body language should send out one unified and powerful message – you are a calm and relaxed person; just like the company you represent! So keep your eyes on the interviewer at all times – check out the colour of their eyes at the start and stay focused on them throughout the interview. Be wary of your hands – keep them still and steady; whether on the desk, or below. Wherever they are to begin with, keep them there – moving them up and down, gesticulating and gesturing, fiddling and picking all tend to distract the audience if they can be seen and have a strangely disconcerting effect when they're not. The camera is on your face in close-up, but the audience can see your shoulders moving and the sound of your hands waving through the air. Do everyone a favour – sit still. And as always, smile. It lights up your face and the studio. Make sure you feel comfortable too. If your seat is too low for you, ask for it to be raised. If it can't and you are behind a desk, ask for a cushion or a telephone directory to sit on; anything to raise you up to a comfortable height and position.

The camera

You must ignore the camera at all times. Too many novice interviewees are torn between talking to the interviewer asking questions and the camera that offers them direct and immediate access to their target audience. As a result, they spend some time looking at the interviewer whilst their mind is thinking about the camera, and the rest of the time trying to impress the watching audience with their warm smiles and well-prepared comments whilst still answering the interviewer. The result is that they look uncomfortable and edgy; shifty even. The eyes dart here and there, the smile looks more like a smirk, and the answers sound over-rehearsed. Look at the interviewer, talk to them, smile at them and answer their questions. The only people who are in that studio so far as you are concerned are the interviewer and you. That camera does not exist! It is the most appalling distraction.

There are other, potential distractions around as well. You may want to take in some form of crib sheet; typically, a postcard with three or four key points printed on it in case you dry-up during the interview. But this will distract you when you're on television; it's there, in your hand, you can feel it, and it's demanding to be looked at! You will, and all the audience will see you do it; and think that you're edgy, nervous, tense or whatever; and this is not the positive image that you want to convey. There may be a carafe or a glass of water on the desk in front of you; and it is tempting to reach for it to wet your rasping throat or to give you a few seconds' thinking time. Don't – you'll find that you'll then want another sip, and another. And you won't find it gives you time to think; you'll just lose the thread of what you're saying and the pace of the interview altogether. Then there is the floor manager and the camera operators, the sound person, and various other technicians – they're all there to distract you. So look at the interviewer – they're incredibly attractive, they've got beautiful eyes; you're going to gaze into them, and let them guide you through this interview. Don't take your eyes off of them!

The end

At the end of the television interview, hold your position – warm, poised and smiling at the interviewer – until you're told that it has finished (or it becomes obvious by the fact that the presenter is getting up, or whatever). Too many first-time interviewees blot a perfectly good interview by letting their eyes wander to the camera at the end (to see if the red light is still on), asking 'Is that it? ('No . . . the camera is still running') or 'Was that okay?' ('No, you've just ruined it') or by standing up and moving away. Just sit there; until you're told to do otherwise. It's far better to experience the minor embarrassment of sitting a moment or two longer than necessary in front of half a dozen people in the studio than the major embarrassment of talking through the end credits in front of a million viewers. And remember, the studio team aren't your customers; the viewers are.

Crisis management tactics

There may be occasions when you have to deal with negative publicity – perhaps your business goes through a difficult patch and has to make some employees redundant, you have to recall a batch of faulty products, or a customer complains to the media about some aspect of your services. It happens; even to the very best of companies. You need to be prepared to handle potentially negative publicity; much of which will involve conducting on-the-spot interviews in the press and on radio and television. Here's what you should do.

Form a crisis management team

A 'crisis management team' is simply a group of people from within a company who will take immediate control of PR activities whenever something goes wrong. Typically, it will comprise the heads of departments – production, marketing, personnel, and so on. In a smaller firm, it may consist of perhaps two of the more senior partners; or even just one person; you! It is important that the team is made up of people in authority who can make major decisions on-the-spot without reference to others; and who have status and credibility within the media, and for the audience. A crisis needs to be seen to be taken seriously; a director who is readily available to answer questions there and then achieves this. A buck passing series of conversations to get to 'someone in marketing' who'll 'ring back after lunch' conveys an indifferent attitude, and the media may well go to town on it; and deservedly so.

Identify all scenarios

Next, the team should discuss everything that could conceivably go wrong – this is another one of those occasions when all of those notes that you composed earlier on will prove their worth; see Chapter 1 pages 5–13 and pages 29–31 in particular. For example, perhaps you know that you are going to have to close one of your unprofitable offices shortly and will have to lose staff – a potential PR problem. Similarly, you know that one or two products from a recent batch of new products have been returned; and you suspect that there is some sort of flaw in the manufacture; again a possible PR difficulty. Some potential problems can be identified relatively easily; by reference to those extensive notes and action checklists (refer to pages 7, 8, 10, 12 and 25). Others are less easy to identify – the employee who doesn't look where they are going and falls down the stairs; and then wants compensation from you, 'or else'. Or the customer who comes into your store and has a heart attack; and perhaps a junior employee doesn't react fast enough, and fails to call an ambulance straightaway. Include as many 'worse-case scenarios' in your discussions as possible. What is your worst business nightmare? Imagine that it's about to happen.

Work through scenarios

You then need to plan out what you will do in varying types of crisis; whether expected or unexpected. You must appoint a media spokesperson who will deal with media enquiries. This needs to be someone senior (not least to show that the firm takes the matter seriously) and who is able to answer questions about the crisis there and then (trying to defer an inter-view until a later time implies that you are ill-prepared, and even evasive). Ideally, the spokesperson will differ according to the nature of the crisis; the personnel director if it is a redundancy, the production manager if it is a product flaw, and so on. Make sure they are available to deal with the media, whether on the telephone, a mobile telephone or preferably, face-to-face. And that they are ready to do it now!

Be positive about each scenario

Whatever problem arises, the media spokesperson should welcome the media in a positive manner; the attitude should be that there is some potentially bad publicity floating around about your company, and the media are now giving you the opportunity to put things right. So help them to do just this; invite them in out of the cold, offer them coffee, let them use your phones or fax machines. Get them on your side. Even if you're one of life's cynics, you should still adopt this approach. They're not going to go away until they've got their story, so you might as well deal with them now and as positively as possible so that you can resolve the matter as best you can. The worst thing that you can do is to delay or (even worse) say 'no comment' – it makes you seem indifferent; and we're all familiar with those damaging press reports that end with a line like 'We approached the such-and-such company but they declined to comment.'

And what was our automatic response (and that of every other reader)? 'They must be guilty!' Don't let your company be put in this position.

Supply all relevant information

Instead, give the media as much information as you can. For example, show them the figures that confirm why you need to make people redundant – you may hate to do this, but it could be the best way to maintain a strong and positive PR image. The more details that you provide for the media, the less they'll have to obtain elsewhere from other, less reliable and biased sources, or (as likely) make up from opinions and suppositions. And always tell the truth – if you're found out about a little white lie, everyone will assume that everything else is a pack of lies as well. Back up your comments whenever possible; and preferably from independent sources. As examples, if you've sold an allegedly faulty product, show copies of the trade body's and local trading standards officer's letters confirming the findings of their examination of it. Your comments are basically seen as biased opinions; those of third parties are viewed as unbiased facts.

Smile – and stay in control of the situation

Remain calm and polite in the face of difficult questions; the media may be trying to unnerve you into losing your cool, and making a rash statement. If the media say 'we've heard that . . .', 'we've been told . . .' or 'one of your customers/ suppliers etc says . . .', you should respond with ' I'm sorry, I can't deal with rumours, let's talk all about the facts.'. The source of their quote is usually non-existent; they're just fishing for a reaction from you. If they ask lots of questions at the same time – another favourite trick of the trade – keep cool, and answer the first question first, then the second, and so on. If they interrupt you with a new question, say 'I'll come to that' and then finish what you were saying. You'll also find that some journalists will not respond at the end of one of your replies – this is one of the oldest tricks in the book. It is designed to unsettle you, to make you fill the silence, to explain further, to justify yourself and to make that rash comment! Don't; you've said what you had to say. Now smile sweetly at them, and wait for them to go on – however long it takes. 'What if?' questions are popular too. For example, 'what will you do if . . .?' and 'What would you say if . . .?' You wouldn't do or say anything at all, because you only deal with facts! A final trick at the end of the interview is to summarize what you said, but in their own words; and incorrectly – they're saying what they want you to say! Stay cool; and correct them.

Add value to the situation

Give added value to everything you say and do. For example, if you're in a redundancy situation, don't just give the media the facts and figures about why your staff have got to be released – show that you've explored all options, have written to competitors to try to find alternative work, have liaised with the Department of Employment and the Department of Social Security, and have sent staff on job-hunting courses, or whatever. Then go another step further to turn the situation to your advantage; see if the media will run a feature on those employees looking for work! And provide follow-up stories for the media – supply back-up press releases and press packs, as appropriate. If one of the employees gets a job before their notice period ends, contact all of those media contacts and tell them all about it.

Following up interviews

You will want to follow up on all of your interviews with the media. First, you will probably want to assess your own performance; but be aware that you are often not the best person to do this, particularly with radio and television interviews. It is a fact that we nearly all dislike the sound of our own voice, thinking that we 'drone on', 'screech' or whatever. But other people don't hear it in this way! Similarly, when we watch ourselves on television, we almost always focus on something trivial, like the way our hair looks, or how we breathed in before we answered a particular question. Yet no-one else has noticed this! So, carry out any self-assessment with other, respected colleagues who will look at your performance in a more objective manner, and suggest improvements for future interviews.

As significant, you will want to appraise the coverage that has been given to your firm, goods and services in the press and on the radio and television. In particular, you will wish to record the dates of coverage; along with places/times, sizes/durations, approaches (particularly if potentially negative interviews have been given) and any immediate and subsequent feedback from your target audience in the form of orders, sales and so forth. (This, after all, is usually the bottom line of most PR activities

ACTION CHECKLIST

MEDIA INTERVIEWS:		MONITORED BY:		DATE:	
INTERVIEW DETAILS	DATE OF COVERAGE	PLACE/TIME	SIZE/DURATION	APPROACH	AUDIENCE FEEDBACK

Figure 3.1 Monitoring media interviews: an action checklist

– to make more sales and increase profits). You may find it useful at this stage to start completing some of the columns of the *Monitoring media interviews: an action checklist* (Figure 3.1).

Ask journalists to let you have a copy of any feature based on your interview; but be prepared to chase this up within a week or two of publication as most journalists will forget, or not bother to forward it. This gives you an opportunity to talk to the journalist again, to develop your working relationship, and perhaps even to plug another story to them. Ask a colleague to listen, watch and record any radio and television interviews that are going out live, or do it yourself if they are being transmitted or broadcast at a later time or date. As time passes, you will begin to build up a clearer and fuller picture of those media that enable you to put your message across to your audience in the way that you want; which publications quote you accurately and fully, which radio stations and television stations edit your interviews without cutting out key comments, and so on. And most important of all, which ones generate the best responses from your target audience. All of this will allow you to assess your PR activities properly, and make amendments and improvements for the coming months.

Organizing press conferences

■　There are three main ways of publicizing your business, products and services to the newspapers, magazines, other publications, radio stations and television stations that will pass on your message to your target audience. These are through press releases, interviews with journalists and presenters – and by organizing press conferences for the media to attend. To do this successfully, you need to know how to:

■　plan a press conference

■　choose a venue, speakers and the invited audience

■　speak in public

■　manage a press conference

■　follow up the event

Planning a press conference

A 'press conference' is simply an event staged by an organization in order to publicize something – a new product launch, for example – to the media; so that they in turn will promote it to their audiences. And hope- fully – if you've done your homework – their audiences and your target audience will be one and the same. To begin with, it's a good idea to take an overview of what is likely to be involved in staging a press conference; before going on to draft and timetable the event.

Overview

You know all about the journalist's 'who-what-when-where-why' maxim for writing a good story – and it provides a useful framework for planning a press conference too. Answer these questions before going any further: they'll give you some idea of what's involved, and what you want to do. Don't worry if you can't answer all of them straightaway; remember, you're taking an overview at the moment.

Who do you think should speak at the press conference? Your mana- ging director, the marketing director or the sales director, perhaps? Who will make the best presentation, answer questions most effectively and be the biggest draw? You may want to have several people present; including the top salesperson to demonstrate a new product, for example. Who do you want to attend the event? This is easier to decide – those contacts on your press list (Figure 2.1, page 38).

What is the aim of this conference? To launch a revamped product? To provide accurate information in response to rumour and speculation in the marketplace? Have this over-riding objective clear in your – and everyone else's – mind. So what is the message that you want to put across to the audience? The key benefits of the new model? The true facts of the matter? It is important that all the speakers are aware of the main message. What do you want the audience to do? To run a news story in the paper? Feature your company, products and services in a radio or television programme? Again, it is essential that everyone is working towards achieving this.

When do you want to stage the press conference? If you have planned your PR activities for some time ahead, you'll know the answer to this question. First time around, you'll probably want at least one month (and preferably more) to set up one successfully – as you'll see over the next few pages, there is a lot of work to do. It can't be done effectively overnight – not to begin with anyway. As significant, when do you not want to hold the event? You might be well advised to avoid those times when competitors are launching new or improved ranges, for example, or at your busiest sales times when sales representatives are better employed out on the road. Again, those notes that you composed so conscientiously will prove invaluable to you here (see Chapter 1).

Where should the conference be held? Many organizations automatically stage their press conferences on their own property; but it is worth considering some alternatives – a hotel or purpose-built conference centre are popular choices as are more unusual venues such as stately homes, theme parks, castles and even ships. Often, these are chosen because they are more prestigious than the company premises, allow an event to be staged without disrupting normal business routines and – now here's the bottom line – they appeal to your media contacts. How many more contacts will come to an event on a ship than to one held in an office block – about three times as many! So your key 'where' question should be 'where would the delegates want the conference to be staged?' Somewhere convenient and accessible, pleasant, and exciting?

Why is the press conference being set up? We've covered the aims and objectives already, when we looked at the 'what' of our 'who-what-when-where-why-how' sequence. But let's stop and consider it again more fully. Why are you really doing it? Because it is the quickest and most effective way of putting across your message; the one most likely to generate the most coverage in the press, or on radio and television? Great – go ahead! But is it being staged to fill a gap in your PR schedule – 'we've nothing planned for that month, so let's try a press conference?' Consider whether it is necessary; and the best way to publicize yourself. There may be less time-consuming and costly ways to achieve the same goals. Perhaps a press release or a series of personal interviews with carefully chosen journalists might be equally successful.

How long should the event last? Bear in mind how much information you have to put across, and how you're going to do that. Typically, a press conference will consist of some form of speech (or speeches), perhaps a demonstration of a new product, and a question and answer session. You need to strike a balance – long enough to put over your message and sell it to them; short enough to maintain the audience's interest. When does your interest start to flag at such events – half-an-hour, maybe an hour at most? Also think about how the conference fits into your overall PR campaign – it's not a stand-alone event; but is part of a campaign; so consider handing out supporting press releases at the end of the conference; and encourage contacts to ask for follow-up interviews.

Drafting and timetabling the event

You may find it helpful to have a theme for your press conference; something that reflects the main message that you're putting across to the audience. If so, make it clear and self-explanatory – 'The Wayliner – Launching an Innovative New Product', for example. Avoid obscure and abstract ones; anything like 'Doing it Right' (Doing what right?) and 'Winning Ways' (What ways?). These simply confuse your potential audience. A straightforward theme can be used to convey your message in pre-event publicity (such as press handouts), may attract your invited audience and can be incorporated into the event itself; on banners, in speeches and in press packs, as examples. It creates a unified and (hopefully) powerful impression; and a long-lasting one too.

Next, think through the activities that will make up the event. Decide exactly what you want to state to your audience. As an example, let's say that you're staging this to promote a revamped range of goods; the most common reason for calling a press conference. You'll want to put over information about the new products, their strengths, unique selling points and benefits for the end users. You'll also probably want to include some facts and figures, technical data and so on. Write everything down – and remember (as always) what your media contacts and their (and hopefully your) audiences want to know. 'What's in it for me?' Identify that – and give them what they want.

You can put across this information in various ways; perhaps an introductory speech about the revised range, a demonstration by your sales team, a question-and-answer session, an examination of the goods by the audience; all rounded off with informal one-to-one conversations between the company representatives and the audience. You may want to provide media contacts with press releases, press packs and/or samples of goods as they leave. Press release and packs make it easier for journalists to write their stories. Be wary of giving away samples too readily though; they can be costly and do not guarantee that your story will be featured in the press or wherever – indeed, some media contacts may attend simply to receive (expensive and/or difficult to obtain) giveaways. (Refer to Chapter 2.)

Consider as well the order of each activity; and their length. With a new product to sell, you may want to have a brief and concise speech, limited time for questions from the floor, and plenty of time for demonstrating and examining the goods. It is wise to help the journalists to get their information as quickly and as easily as possible; so have fewer speeches, and more question-and-answer sessions as a general rule. Stress the benefits for end users – in speeches, answers, informal discussions and so forth. Keep all that technical data and specifications to a minimum – most people aren't interested; and those that are can ask. Put all the boring bits in an extra information sheet in the press packs – to be referred to or disposed of by the media contacts, as appropriate.

Finally, think about any social activities that you want to incorporate in the press conference; typically, you'll want to provide tea and coffee for the audience on their arrival; and perhaps sandwiches and wine, fruit juices and so on at the end, whilst company representatives are mingling with the media contacts. Never under-estimate the importance of these activities; they give you a chance to meet your contacts face-to-face and to chat to them. You may only have spoken to some of them on the phone before – this now gives you the opportunity to build on your relationship in an informal and relaxed setting.

Choosing venues, speakers and the invited audience

As soon as you've drafted out a timetabled programme for your press conference, you can move on to the three key ingredients – the venue, the speakers and the audience. Here's what you need to know about them.

Venues

When choosing where to hold your press conference, you should start by identifying your selection criteria against which locations and venues can be assessed. The location – town, city or wherever – needs to be convenient and accessible for your media contacts. If your business is sited in Surrey or Kent but all the media representatives are based in London, then it is sensible to stage the press conference in that city. The venue – whether your business premises, a hotel or wherever – has to be suitable and large

PRESS CONFERENCE: VENUE REQUIREMENTS		NUMBER:	
		DATE:	
ADMINISTRATIVE HELP	☐	NOTEPAPER	☐
BLINDS	☐	PARKING	☐
BOARDS	☐	PENS/PENCILS	☐
CAMCORDERS	☐	PHOTOCOPIERS	☐
CASSETTE RECORDERS	☐	PODIA	☐
CHAIRS	☐	POINTERS	☐
CLOAKROOMS	☐	PROJECTORS	☐
COMPUTER TERMINALS	☐	SAFES	☐
CURTAINS	☐	SCREENS	☐
DISABLED FACILITIES	☐	SECRETARIAL HELP	☐
DISPLAY BOARDS	☐	SHREDDERS	☐
EXTENSION LEADS	☐	SOCKETS	☐
FAX MACHINES	☐	STAGES	☐
FOYER	☐	TABLES	☐
HEATING	☐	TECHNICIANS	☐
INTERPRETERS	☐	TELEPHONES	☐
KITCHEN	☐	TELEVISIONS	☐
LECTERNS	☐	TOILETS	☐
LIFTS	☐	TRIPODS	☐
LIGHTING	☐	VIDEO PLAYERS	☐
MEDICAL SERVICES	☐	VIDEO RECORDERS	☐
MICROPHONES	☐	WALL COVERINGS	☐
OTHER	☐	OTHER	☐
OTHER	☐	OTHER	☐
OTHER	☐	OTHER	☐
COMPILED BY:		SIGNATURE:	

Figure 4.1 Venue facilities and services: an action checklist

enough to accommodate the speakers, equipment and the audience. It must be easy-to-access by participants; and equipment. It is not unknown for conference organizers to book a venue; and discover later that they cannot get their display models through the doors. You will also have a limit to the amount you can pay out to stage a press conference. Of course, you may also have a whole host of other queries according to your specific circumstances – see *Venue facilities and services: an action checklist* (Figure 4.1) for some useful ideas.

With the right location established (London, Manchester, Harrogate or wherever), you can set about picking an appropriate venue. If your business property fulfils all of your criteria, then it seems sensible to hold the conference there – assuming that this will not disrupt the smooth running of your business. It is by far the easiest option – and there's nothing wrong with that as long as it's the right one too. Alternatively, you'll need to look around. You may know potentially suitable hotels or conference centres or can seek advice from trade associations, chambers of commerce and other professional contacts that you've built up over the years. In particular, the British Association of Conference Towns (BACT), the Association of Conference Executives (ACE) and the Meetings Industry Association (MIA) can offer practical assistance (refer to the Useful Contacts section). Benn's *Conference Blue Book* and *Conference Green Book* are helpful publications listing thousands of conference venues across the United Kingdom. See the Further Reading section for details.

Visit possible venues to make your choice. See if the person responsible for hiring out rooms seems competent; and that you have confidence in their ability to do their job and deliver. As examples, are they experienced in this field? Have they helped stage press conferences before? A useful pointer is whether or not they make constructive suggestions; or just agree with what you say. Go into the rooms – check entrances, heights, lengths, widths, power points, lighting, heating, ventilation, noise levels, facilities and services. Check that any other criteria are met. Is the venue available on the chosen date; and what is the best deal that you can get from the venue? Make sure you can come in on budget.

Once you've found your preferred venue, you can make a provisional booking. Those venues that are used to staging conferences will probably produce two documents for you to read, and agree to – a 'conditions of hire' form and a 'code of practice'. Examples of these are reproduced as Figure 4.2 and Figure 4.3 respectively; you'll find them informative reading at this point. In essence, check through the conditions of hire and make sure you are happy to abide by them. If not, you'll need to negotiate, or go elsewhere. Similarly, look through the code of practice and ensure you feel comfortable with what you're being asked to agree with before going ahead. If all's well, you can move on to complete a booking form – a typical example is shown as Figure 4.4. Note its contents; they're fairly standard for the industry.

It's a good idea to attach an accompanying letter to a booking form, confirming anything that's been agreed verbally, and is not otherwise stated in writing. Cover your back. For example, their conference executive may have agreed to allowing you free rehearsal time or the use of a technician

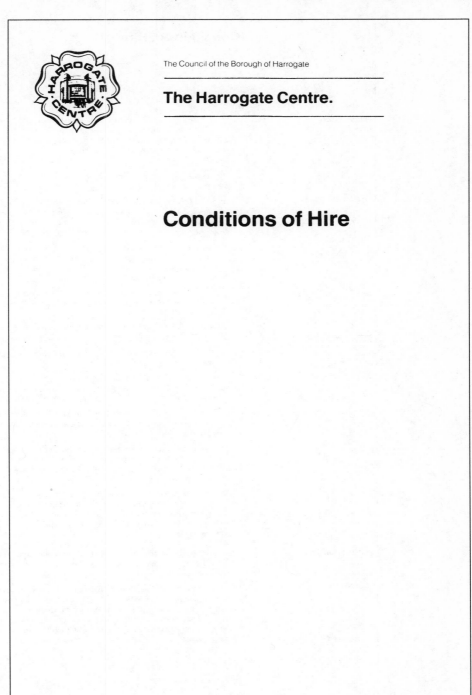

The Council of the Borough of Harrogate

The Harrogate Centre.

Conditions of Hire

Figure 4.2   Sample conditions of hire form

Conditions of Hire

Interpretation

1. Throughout these Conditions where reference is made to any statute, regulations, byelaw or otherwise by name or implication these Conditions shall be read, construed and take effect as if they referred by name to the respective statute, regulations, byelaw or otherwise in force at the date of the Hiring Agreement including any amendments then current.

Throughout these Conditions the following expressions shall have the meanings assigned to them:

"Basic staffing complement" means one stage manager, one sound engineer, one lighting engineer, one front of house manager and a maximum of four doormen; for concerts a sufficient number of usherettes will be included; and basic staffing will be construed accordingly.

"Centre" means the Harrogate Centre or any part and includes all rooms, halls, corridors, lifts, stairways, cloakrooms, lavatories, and conveniences used or to be used by a Hirer or person authorised by him on the occasion of any hiring but does not include the restaurant, kitchen or bars.

"The Council" means the Council of the Borough of Harrogate including any Committee, Sub-Committee or Officer appointed by the Council for the purpose of management of the Harrogate Centre.

"Director" means the Council's Director of Resort Services for the time being or any person authorised by the Director or the Council to act on his behalf.

"Function" includes any kind of event or purpose for which the Centre is to be used by the Hirer.

"Hirer" means the person who has made application (whether personally or through an agent) to use the Centre and includes his agent and any other person employed by him (whether as servant or independent contractor) or acting under his direction.

"Hiring Agreement" means the agreement entered into between the Council and the Hirer setting out the period of hire and other details and incorporating these Conditions of Hire by reference.

"Hiring charge" means the sum ascertainable from the Hiring Agreement as the cost of hire of the Centre and does not include any additional costs to be charged as a result of requests made to the Director under these Conditions or otherwise unless the contrary appears from the Hiring Agreement.

"Period of hire" means the time during which the Hirer has contractual license to use the Centre under the Hiring Agreement including the period during which he requires access to make all preparations necessary for the function, the duration of the function and the time agreed thereafter for removing all materials, equipment etc. used for the purposes of the function.

Details of function

2. A complete programme of the function shall be delivered to the Director as soon as possible and in any case not less than seven days before the commencement of the period of hire.

In the event of the Hirer wishing to promote an exhibition he must submit a scale plan of the proposed layout of the exhibition to the Director for approval before agreements are made with the exhibitors. The plan will be submitted by the Director to the County Fire Officer for approval. No alterations may be made to the plan after it has been approved by the Director except with his written permission and the exhibition shall be laid out and maintained entirely in accordance with the approved plan.

3

Figure 4.2 Sample conditions of hire form (continued)

Conditions of Hire

The Hirer shall notify the Director in writing not less than twelve weeks before the date of the function if it is intended to show films or video tapes at the function. Details must be given as to the type of film stock and projection equipment and/or video tape and recorder which it is proposed to use and whether members of the audience will be charged for admission either by programme or ticket. No entertainment for which a licence under the Cinematograph Acts is required may be given in the Centre unless the Hirer has first obtained the requisite licence. The Hirer shall be responsible for ensuring compliance with the terms of such licence.

In the event of the Centre being used by the Hirer for a conference the numbers of delegates who attended shall be supplied by the Hirer to the Director not more than seven days after the final day of that conference.

Advertising

3. If the Director so requires, the Hirer shall submit to him a draft of any poster, notice, bill, programme, announcement, advertisement or invitation relating to a function for which the Centre has been hired and shall comply with all requirements which the Director may reasonably impose.

No posters, notices or bills may be displayed inside or outside the Centre except by permission of the Director. The display of a reasonable number of approved posters or notices will be permitted on condition that the affixing and removal of same shall in no way affect, mark or damage the materials, fabric or decoration of the Centre internally or externally.

Tickets

4. Advance ticket sales shall be undertaken by the Director at the Centre Box Office and/or other offices under the control of the Council for all functions to which the general public is to be admitted unless the Hirer has obtained written permission to the contrary from the Director.

The Box Office in the Centre shall be manned by Council staff, unless written consent to the contrary has been obtained from the Director, and the Hirer shall pay for their services at the rates in force at the date of the Hiring Agreement.

When tickets are to be sold under this Condition printing will be undertaken by the Director at the expense of the Hirer.

In the case of functions so approved for the purposes of this Condition by the Director, the Hirer will be permitted to arrange the printing and sale of his own tickets. In such cases the tickets must conform to a prescribed pattern, details of which can be obtained from the Director.

The number of complimentary tickets to be issued by the Hirer for any function shall be subject to agreement by the Director.

Reservations for the Council

5. The Hirer shall reserve for the Council seats A1-A4 in Block E, seats A10-A13 in Block F and seats H1-H14 in Block G, all seat numbers inclusive, in respect of any function to which the general public is to be admitted and the Hirer shall deliver to the Director as soon as they are received from the printers the tickets for the seats which have been so reserved.

Care of the Centre

6. The Hirer may not place on or affix to the outside or inside of the Centre or bring into the Centre any furniture, fittings or temporary structures, except with the written permission of the Director.

Where the Centre is used for an exhibition all stands shall be of modular construction and approved by the Director in advance. No painting of stands or displays shall be permitted within the Centre. Where any machinery is to be displayed adequate protection must be afforded to walls and floor coverings in order to prevent wear and tear and damage from leakage or otherwise.

4

Figure 4.2 Sample conditions of hire form (continued)

Conditions of Hire

In no circumstances shall any nails, screws, staples or pins of any kind be fixed into any part of the Centre, or its furniture, fittings or fixtures. Nothing may be displayed on or affixed to the walls of the Centre without the consent of the Director.

On termination of the hiring for any reason whatsoever whether before or after the function for which the Centre has been hired all machinery, equipment, furniture, fittings, stalls, stands, displays or other materials or exhibits brought into the Centre for the purposes of the function or displayed on or affixed to any part of the Centre shall be removed by the Hirer in such a way that no part of the Centre its fixtures, fittings or decoration whether internal or external is affected, marked or damaged in any way and any part of the Centre its fixtures, fittings or decoration which is so affected, marked or damaged shall be restored by the Council to the condition in which it was at the time of commencement of the period of hire and the cost to the Council of such restoration will be recharged to the Hirer.

Electrical Wiring and Fittings

7. The Hirer shall not interfere, nor permit any interference with any of the electrical wiring, installations or fittings of the Centre.

No electrical or other wiring (e.g. telephone - shortwave - amplification etc.) or electrical or other equipment or apparatus of any kind is to be placed in the Centre without the prior written consent of the Director.

Directional adjustment of the foyer light fittings will be carried out by the Council at the request of the Hirer and the cost of such adjustment and readjustment to the original setting will be charged to the Hirer at the rates in force at the date of the Hiring Agreement.

Where not already provided in the Centre a three-phase supply will be laid on by the Council at the request of the Hirer and the cost will be charged to the Hirer at the rates in force at the date of the Hiring Agreement.

Fire Precautions

8. All scenery, effects, properties, cloths, materials, stands and decorative displays must be rendered and maintained non-inflammable and must be declared to and approved by the County Fire Officer or his representative not less than seven days before the start of the function for which the Centre has been hired.

Any effects, properties, cloths, materials, stands and decorative displays which cannot be rendered non-inflammable under the preceding paragraph shall be declared to the Chief Fire Officer not less than one month before the period of hire commences and the Hirer shall comply with any requirement or recommendation of the Chief Fire Officer in respect of such effects, properties, cloths, materials, stands and decorative displays affecting safety, fire prevention or related matters.

Seating

9. The Centre is let with full seating and the Hirer will be responsible for all costs incurred in the removal, storage and replacement of any seating not required for the Hirer's function at the rates in force at the date of the Hiring Agreement.

The Council will use its best endeavours to arrange seating in accordance with the Hirer's requirements provided reasonable notice of such requirements has been given to the Director.

The Hirer must not issue tickets for admission to the function in excess of the seating capacity of the Centre for that function. In no circumstances may the Hirer admit to the function a greater number of persons than the number of seats provided in the Centre for that function.

Where the Director considers it to be necessary to fix a limit to the number of persons to be admitted to any function, the Hirer must not admit a greater number of persons than that specified by the Director.

5

Figure 4.2 Sample conditions of hire form (continued)

Conditions of Hire

Compliance with Statutes etc.

10. The Hirer shall comply fully with all statutes. rules, regulations, orders, byelaws, or other requirements whether for ensuring public order, safety or decency or for any other purpose whatsoever affecting the use of the Centre for the purpose for which it has been hired, and with all requirements of the Health and Safety Executive. of the Police and Fire Authorities and of the Council including these Conditions and the duty to obtain all licences, consents and approvals necessary for the function.

    All obligations, stipulations and Conditions to be observed on the part of the Hirer shall apply equally to the Hirer's servants, agents, contractors, sub-licensees and visitors (insofar as the same are relevant) and the Hirer shall be responsible for ensuring their compliance.

Right of Entry

11. The Council reserves for the Director the right of entry to the Centre during the period of hire to view the premises. the arrangements made for the proper supervision of the function and for any other reason or purpose which he may think proper in the interests of the Council, the Centre or Council staff.

Good Order

12. No impropriety of language, dress, dance, gesture or personality shall be permitted at any function and the Hirer shall to the best of his ability maintain and keep good order and decent behaviour in the Centre throughout the period of hire.

    The Council reserves the right for the Director to refuse admission to, or to remove from the Centre any person who, in his opinion, is disorderly or objectionable.

    The Hirer must inform every entertainer or group of entertainers that his or their performance must not be conducted in such a way that it may incite the audience to behave in a manner which may result in damage to the property of the Council or in a breach of public order, safety regulations or these Conditions and that members of the audience are not permitted to dance in the gangways or between the seats, but must remain seated throughout the performance.

Staffing

13. (a) Basic staffing will be provided at the Centre by the Council for the duration of the period of hire or as considered necessary by the Director.

    Any staff required by the Hirer in addition to the basic staffing complement if requested in writing not less than seven days before the date of the function will be provided at the cost of the Hirer at the rates in force at the date of the Hiring Agreement.

    (b) The Hirer must provide, at his own expense, Stewards of such a number as the Director may consider necessary for the proper conduct of the function.

    All Stewards must be and remain on duty at the Centre for the period specified by the Director and must be instructed that they are to comply with any requirement of the Director.

    (c) For all functions in the Centre to which the general public is to be admitted the Director will provide a sufficient number of trained Security Personnel to meet the demands of the particular function as anticipated by the Director in consultation with the Hirer but in default of agreement as fixed by the Director. Security Personnel will be provided at the cost of the Hirer at the rates in force at the date of the Hiring Agreement.

    (d) At the discretion of the Director cloakroom facilities with attendants will be provided.

    (e) If the Hirer shall so request the Director he shall use his best endeavours to provide any additional staff notwithstanding that it may be outside normal working hours and the Council shall be entitled to charge for such staff at the rates in force at the date of the Hiring Agreement.

Police and Firemen

14. The Hirer will be charged for any attendance of the Police or Fire Service which the Director shall judge to be necessary.

6

Figure 4.2 Sample conditions of hire form (continued)

Conditions of Hire

Collections

15. The collection of money whether for charitable or any other purpose from those attending the function is not permitted without the prior written consent of the Director.

Sales of chattels and programmes

16. No chattel or real property may be raffled, sold or offered for sale whether by auction or otherwise in the Centre, with the following exceptions:

(a) the sale of programmes catalogues or other literature or articles ancillary to the function.

(b) where the sale of chattels or real property is the express or implied object of the function.

(c) sales expressly authorised in writing by the Director prior to the function.

Rates of commission on all sales must be approved by the Director prior to the function.

Copyright

17. No copyright work shall be performed other than

(a) such as is authorised by the current licence of the Performing Rights Society Limited a copy of which can be inspected at the Centre on request and shall be deemed to have been read by the Hirer,

(b) any work in respect of which the licence of the owner of the copyright for the performance is produced to the Director before the commencement of the function, and the Hirer shall indemnify the Council against all costs, claims and liability in respect of the performance of any copyright work not so authorised.

For the purpose of this clause "copyright" includes the copyright subsisting in a film video tape recording or broadcast as such but not the copyright subsisting in a recording (not being a film video tape recording or broadcast) as such. References to the performance of a copyright work shall be deemed to include the playing or reproduction of the work by means of a recording or any other means whatsoever.

A Hirer shall, within seven days of the date of a function, render the Director a return in duplicate on the form provided of all works performed in the Centre during the period of hire.

Amplification and relay equipment

18. A Hirer who wishes to make use of any equipment installed in the Centre for the purpose of sound amplification or relaying shall make arrangements for the same with the Director.

Recording/reproduction broadcast etc. of entertainment.

19. The Hirer must not record, transmit or broadcast, or permit to be recorded, transmitted or broadcast by telegraph, telephone, radio, television, video tape or any other means, any performance, entertainment, or the subject matter of any function, except with the previous written consent of the Director and on such terms as may be approved by him.

The Hirer must not reproduce whether aurally or visually, or permit the aural or visual reproduction of any performance or entertainment or the subject matter of any function except with the prior written permission of the Director and on such terms as may be approved by him.

No photograph, film or video tape recording may be taken or made in the Centre without the prior written permission of the Director and on such terms as may be approved by him.

Refreshments

20. The Council reserves for its own exclusive benefit all bars and refreshment rooms with the right to sell and provide all refreshments whether solid or liquid including wines beers, spirits and other alcoholic liquors to be consumed in the Centre and to provide such catering facilities as it may in its absolute discretion think fit.

Cleaning

21. (a) The Hirer will leave the Centre and all its fittings, fixtures, furniture, apparatus and equipment in a reasonably clean condition. If the Director is not satisfied with the condition of the Centre or the said fittings, fixtures, furniture, apparatus and equipment at the expiration of the period of hire, the Hirer will be required to reimburse the Council for the cost of cleaning to a standard satisfactory to the Director.

7

Figure 4.2 Sample conditions of hire form (continued)

Conditions of Hire

(b) The Hirer will be required to ensure that all structures, goods and chattels erected in or brought into the Centre during the period of hire and all residual rubbish and debris are removed from the Centre by the expiration of the period of hire so that the Centre when vacated is left in a clean and orderly state. In the event of the Hirer failing to comply with his obligations under this Condition the Council or the Director shall be entitled to put the Centre into a clean and orderly state and, where necessary, to place any such structures, goods and chattels in store and the cost to the Council of securing compliance with this Condition will be charged to the Hirer as an additional charge including any transportation and storage costs.

Exclusion of Liability

22. The Council will not be responsible for any article of any kind which is brought into or left in the Centre.

Where the Hirer is in breach of his obligations under Condition 21 and the Director is thereby required to exercise his powers under 21(b) the Hirer shall not hold the Council or the Director responsible in any way for any loss which may occur to the Hirer due to any failure on the part of the Director to distinguish between items requiring storage and items requiring destruction.

Any structures, goods or chattels which are placed in store under Condition 21 will be held by the Council to the order of the Hirer and at his sole risk.

Indemnity

23. The Hirer will be liable for any damage done to or loss of any property of the Council or for which the Council is responsible under the law, arising out of the hire of the Centre whether caused by the Hirer or by any other persons using the Centre as a result of the Hiring Agreement.

Liability under this Condition shall exclude loss or damage caused to the building (but not its fixtures, fittings or equipment) to the extent that it is insured by the Council.

In the event of any damage or loss being sustained, suffered or incurred by the Hirer or any other person due to any breakdown of machinery, failure of supply of electricity, leakage of water, fire, government restriction or act of God or to the temporary closing of the Centre or the interruption of the period of hire by circumstances beyond the control of the Council or to any other cause whatsoever the Hirer shall accept full responsibility and shall indemnify the Council against all costs, claims, demands and expenses arising. Provided that this Condition shall not apply to personal injury, damage or loss or to any claim caused by the negligence of any servant of the Council arising out of the performance of his duties as such servant.

Insurance

24. Without prejudice to the generality of Condition 10 to comply with all statutes, rules, regulations, orders, byelaws or other requirements whether for public safety or otherwise and without prejudice to the generality of the other Conditions relating to the liability of the Hirer to the Council for the conduct of the function and the care of the Centre its fixtures fittings and equipment, the Hirer shall procure public liability insurance cover for the period of hire in the sum of four million pounds and shall produce evidence to the Director not less than seven days before the commencement of the period of hire.

Anticipatory Breach

25. The Council reserves the right to cancel any function if in the opinion of the Director:
    (a) the Hirer intends to use the Centre for any purpose other than the purpose specified in the Hiring Agreement.

    (b) the Hirer intends to use the Centre for a public entertainment in respect of which a licence under the Cinematograph Acts is required, and the Hirer has not obtained the requisite licence.

    (c) the function may lead to a breach of the peace or acts of violence may occur or damage may be caused to the Centre or any of its fixtures, fittings or decoration.

    (d) the nature of the function or of any item in the programme is such as to render it undesirable that it should be in a building under the control of the Council.

8

Figure 4.2 Sample conditions of hire form (continued)

Conditions of Hire

In the event of the function being cancelled as provided above, or being cancelled by the Hirer in circumstances in which the Council is unable to re-let the Centre, the Council reserves the right:

(a) to retain any deposit or sum of money that may have been paid by the Hirer; and

(b) to claim any balance of the hiring charge payable under the Hiring Agreement; and

(c) to claim any other expenses incurred by the Council in connection with the function.

Cancellation by the Director

26. The Council reserves the right to cancel any function if in the opinion of the Director:

(a) it is necessary to close the Centre for the purpose of executing urgent repairs.

(b) it is in the public interest that the Centre shall be closed on any day for which the function has been arranged.

(c) the Centre has been rendered unfit for use by reason of flood, tempest, storm, fire, electrical or mechanical breakdown or other cause beyond the Council's control.

(d) the Centre is required for some public or civic purpose. (As far as possible periods of hire will be arranged so as not to conflict with civic requirements).

(e) there is in existence an industrial dispute rendering the holding of the function inadvisable.

In the event of any function being cancelled as provided above, the Hirer shall be repaid any deposit or sum of money that may have been paid for the period of the cancellation but shall have no claim against the Council for any damage or loss which he may sustain or have sustained nor in respect of any liability which he may incur or have incurred in consequence of such cancellation.

Cancellation by the Hirer

27. If the Hirer shall cancel the function the Council shall be entitled to the whole of the hiring charge together with a sum equal to any costs borne by the Council in connection with the function up to the date of the Hirer's cancellation Provided Always that if notice of the cancellation is received by the Council prior to the date on which the period of hire would otherwise have commenced then if the Council shall find another Hirer for the whole or part of the Centre the Hirer shall be liable to pay only for that part of the Centre and only for that period of hire which have not been taken over by such other Hirer.

Breach of Conditions of Hire

28. In the event of the Hirer failing to observe and perform or failing to cause to be observed and performed any of these Conditions the Council may, without prejudice to any right of action which it may have against the Hirer, forthwith and without prior notice to the Hirer cancel the function and, if necessary, require him to vacate the Centre and in the event of any function being cancelled the Council shall be entitled to retain any deposit or other payments he may have made and the Hirer shall have no claim against the Council for any damage or loss he may sustain or have sustained nor in respect of any liability which he may incur or have incurred in consequence of such cancellation.

Bankruptcy etc.

29. In the event of a Hirer committing any act of bankruptcy or (being a Company) entering into liquidation either compulsorily or voluntarily the function shall be automatically cancelled and in the event of any function being so cancelled the Council shall be entitled to retain any deposit or sum of money that may have been paid and the Hirer his Trustee in Bankruptcy, Receiver or Liquidator shall have no claim against the Council in respect of such cancellation or any damage or loss which he may sustain or have sustained nor in respect of any liability which he may incur or have incurred in consequence of such cancellation.

9

Figure 4.2 Sample conditions of hire form (continued)

COUNCIL OF THE BOROUGH OF HARROGATE

CODE OF PRACTICE FOR USE OF
HARROGATE INTERNATIONAL CONFERENCE CENTRE

The following service as reinforcement to the Conditions of Hire issued with the Contract for your use of the Conference Centre. Not all items necessarily apply to your event but must be adhered to when appropriate. (There is no particular order of priority to this list).

1   No signs, notices or posters to be affixed to the internal fabric of the building – all such signs/notices to be free-standing. In exceptional circumstances, Blu-tac or similar substances may be used on glass surfaces with the prior permission of the Event Manager responsible for your event. NB: 'Sticky-Pads' are *NOT* acceptable at all. Permission to erect/display exterior signs must also be sought from the Event Manager.

2   Painting of construction materials/exhibition stands is prohibited in all carpeted areas. Where this is necessary in the Auditorium during set construction, steps *MUST BE* taken to protect the flooring by use of suitable material, e.g. plastic sheeting. N.B. Painting is not allowed at all in the two foyer levels.

3   Sections of stage sets/lighting rigs *MUST NOT* be placed on the backs of Auditorium seating whilst awaiting use – they should, where possible, be placed on the floor. If, however, sheer size restricts this, suitable protection *MUST BE* placed on the seating in question and only under guidance by the Department of Resort Services Stage Manager.

4   Any scaffolding or other temporary structures/platforms *CAN ONLY* be constructed in seated areas using previously approved materials under the supervision of Department of Resort Services technical staff.

5   The utmost care *MUST BE* taken when transporting equipment and containers around the building, especially with regard to doors, doorways, stairways, corridor walls and carpeted areas. Particular care must be taken when it is necessary to transfer

Figure 4.3 Sample code of practice

stand materials between the two foyer levels using either the ramp or the escalator, as ceiling levels vary quite significantly. Please note weight limit in the two passenger lifts (900 kg each) – any costs incurred due to overloading will be recharged.

6   The permanently let display cases on both foyer levels must not be obscured by stands or display materials; and the mobile catering/bar counters situated in these foyers may only be used with the permission of the Department of Resort Services Commerical Manager. Display materials, banners, etc. must not be attached to the window blinds in these two areas under any circumstances.

7   Cooking *IS NOT* allowed inside the building other than in the purpose-built kitchen attached to the Centre Restaurant and under the strict control of the Commercial Manager or the Buffet Area in Exhibition Hall D, if available. Any other arrangements must take place outside, in suitable vehicles. This applies particularly to crew catering connected with travelling entertainment events.

8   Food and drink *CANNOT* be consumed in the Auditorium at any time, including build-up and breakdown periods. Areas are provided back-stage for crew refreshments breaks.

9   Fire exist signs *MUST NOT* be obscured. If the construction of a stage set is such that the exits on either side of the stage are covered, access *MUST BE* allowed around either end of the set and temporary directional signs fitted.

10 All aisles *MUST* remain free from encumbrance whilst delegates/ audience occupy the Auditorium.

11 The unauthorised parking of vehicles on the paved area between the main entrance and the flagpoles is *STRICTLY PROHIBITED*.

Any damage caused to the fabric, furniture or fittings of the Conference Centre as a consequence of failure to observe these conditions will be restored by the Department of Resort Services and the cost recharged to the organiser of the event.

Figure 4.3   Sample code of practice (continued)

COMPANY LOGO

BOOKING FORM

Organisation/Name of Group _____

Name and Title of Organiser _____

Daytime Telephone Number of Organiser _____

Fax Number of Organiser _____

Full Address _____

_____

_____ Postcode _____

Date of Arrival _____ Date of Departure _____

Time of Arrival _____ Time of Departure _____

Number of people attending _____

Number of bedrooms required: Twin Rooms _____ Single Rooms _____

Training Room required from (day and time) _____

Training Room required until (day and time) _____

The Training Room will be required for _____ people

How would you like the Training Room to be set out? (please tick)

U-shape formation *with* tables ☐
U-shape formation *without* tables ☐
In a square *with* tables ☐
In a square *without* tables ☐
Theatre style ☐

Do you have any further instructions regarding the layout of the training room?

_____

If you would like a particular Training Room, *if available*, please specify

_____

Will you require any Seminar Rooms, if so how many and when?
(£50.00 per day)

_____

*Contact name
and address,
Tel, Fax and
email nos.*

Figure 4.4 Sample venue booking form

Equipment
If you would like the use of any equipment during your stay, please tick appropriate boxes.

16mm film projector ☐

Overhead projector ☐

35mm carousel projector ☐

Flip chart ☐

Whiteboard ☐

VHS video recorder + TV ☐

Do you have any further requirements? _____

_____

_____

Meals and Refreshments (please refer to "Catering Arrangements" on Page One).
Please tick appropriate boxes and insert times you would like tea/coffee to be served. Thank you.

	Breakfast 8.00-8.30 am *Please tick*	Coffee/Tea and Biscuits *Please insert time*	Lunch 1.00 pm *Please tick*	Packed Lunch *Please tick*	Tea/Coffee and Biscuits *Please insert time*	Pre-Dinner Bar *Please tick*	Dinner 6.00 pm *Please tick*	Evening Bar *Please tick*
FRI								
SAT								
SUN								
MON								
TUES								
WED								
THUR								
FRI								
SAT								

How did you first find out about the hall? _____

If you have stayed at the Hall before, during which year did you stay? _____

I have read and understand the Conditions of Booking.

Signed _____   Date _____

Please return the completed form, together with your deposit or official order to:

Telephone: Fax:
Please make your cheque payable to:

Figure 4.4 Sample venue booking form (continued)

CONTINUATION SHEET

**PLEASE INDICATE WHETHER SINGLE OR TWIN ROOMS ARE REQUIRED
AND BRACKET TOGETHER THOSE PEOPLE WHO ARE TO SHARE**

Male/ Female	FULL NAME (please print clearly)	CATEGORY OF ROOM REQUIRED	SPECIAL DIETS/ (vegetarian, vegan, etc.) MEDICAL CONDITIONS

Figure 4.4 Sample venue booking form (continued)

GROUP BOOKINGS - LIST OF *NON-RESIDENT* DELEGATES

NAME OF GROUP _____

DATES OF VISIT _____

FULL NAME (please print clearly)	TIME OF ARRIVAL	TIME OF DEPARTURE	SPECIAL DIETS (vegetarian, vegan etc.)

Figure 4.4 Sample venue booking form (continued)

GROUP BOOKINGS - LIST OF RESIDENT DELEGATES

NAME OF GROUP _____

DATES OF VISIT _____

PLEASE INDICATE WHETHER SINGLE OR TWIN ROOMS ARE REQUIRED
AND BRACKET TOGETHER THOSE PEOPLE WHO ARE TO SHARE

Male/ Female	FULL NAME (please print clearly)	CATEGORY OF ROOM REQUIRED	SPECIAL DIETS/ (vegetarian, vegan, etc.) MEDICAL CONDITIONS

Please return this section of the Booking Form (together with a course programme if you have one) as soon as possible.

Please return to:
Tel: Fax:

CONTINUATION SHEET ATTACHED

Figure 4.4 Sample venue booking form (continued)

to operate a video player. Request a written response agreeing to your requirements; especially those that vary significantly from the conditions of hire. You may then receive a booking confirmation for your press conference. The best advice here is to check it line-by-line to make certain each is 100 per cent correct; it is surprising how many mistakes are included in some official confirmations. Correct anything in writing and respond promptly. Notify any changes to your plans as you go. Check all is in order at the venue a week before the event is due to be held. On the day, arrive first; at least half-an-hour before anyone else. Be there to supervise and handle any problems that arise.

Speakers

Ideally, the people who are going to speak at your conference, demonstrate a product or whatever, need to have certain attributes. They should be wholly familiar with their subject; and know what they are talking about. For example, you can be sure that a journalist on a trade publication will ask some obscure question about specifications. It needs to be answered by the person speaking; so make sure they can. They also need to be experienced and capable of doing what you want them to do. If a product has to be demonstrated, choose someone who is used to doing this – it isn't always as easy as it sounds. They may need to be well-known in the trade or industry as well; and respected by the audience. A popular speaker acts as a draw; people will come to listen and talk to them.

In practice, you'll probably have some idea of who you want to take part in the event; typically, the MD to take the 'chair', the marketing manager to speak, the most experienced salesperson to demonstrate, and perhaps the production manager to handle technical questions. You will usually act in a supervisory role; making certain that everything runs smoothly. You need to make sure at an early stage that your speakers are all going to be available to attend the press conference. And it's worth thinking about the consequences of attendance too. As an example, the salesperson will have to come off the road for that day – so decide whether the benefits of being at this event outweigh any losses incurred by being off the road.

It is essential that everyone participating in the press conference is totally familiar in advance with what is happening and when, what they are doing and what everybody else is doing too. You do not want anyone – typically the MD – turning up on the day ready to give an off-the-cuff speech that (brilliant though it may be) is inconsistent with the rest of the speeches, comments made and answers given. So make certain that they all know the following; date, start and finish times, location, theme and aims, who is saying and doing what and when, the main message for media contacts, the main message for their readers, listeners and viewers, and miscellaneous details (refreshments, press giveaways, and anything you can think of that is relevant to your situation). Get everyone together well in advance to discuss this, memo changes and developments to all participants as you proceed and most important of all, rehearse the event.

The invited audience

The core of your audience at a press conference should comprise all of those journalists and presenters who are on that media contacts list that you drew up when you were writing and sending out press releases. See Figure 2.1 on page 38. You may find that you are expected to invite others – the MD might play golf with the editor of a particular newspaper, some customers and/or suppliers could want to come along – and it may be diplomatic to invite them; but it's your press list that's all important. These people are the ones that are most likely to enable you to put across your PR message in the way that you want to your target audience.

You should personally invite your contacts to attend. Telephone them in the first instance. This is always more effective than a letter or a press release which may go astray or might not be read in time. Also, it's hard to ignore or refuse a verbal invitation; and a conversation gives you the chance to 'sell' your story to them. Before you call, decide what it is that will make them attend – perhaps your firm is a prestigious one and its views are considered important in the industry, the topic may be a hot, 'must-know' matter, the speaker might be renowned in the industry; or maybe there is a more simple, base explanation. It offers a break from the office, a chance to meet old friends, the opportunity to visit an unusual location, and to pick up some freebies.

The reality is that your contacts will probably have a mix of motives; but there should be one over-riding one – it's the chance to get an easy-to-write story of interest to their audience. That's what you're selling. So, the information that you're going to put across in this call will concentrate on why this new product will be of benefit to their readers, listeners and viewers; and how you can make it easy for your media contact to produce a news story or feature: products on display will enable them to examine the goods, experts will be available for discussion purposes, and so forth. Stress (albeit diplomatically) that information can only be obtained by attending; otherwise, some will suggest that you simply fax or e-mail material for them to consider. That's not good enough – they've got to be there! Draw in the other reasons for attending – that great guest speaker, former colleagues will be present, or whatever. But do this subtly – these may be unspoken reasons.

Of course, some facts and figures – dates, times, places, as examples – will be mentioned in your telephone conversation. These – and others – will then need to be provided in a follow-up letter. Here's what needs to be covered: date, start time, end time, location, theme and purpose, guest speakers, key benefits for the audience (chance to meet guest speakers, see new range, etc., as examples), main benefits for their audiences (cheaper goods, more versatility, durability, as examples), other attractions (unusual location, refreshments, press packs, samples, etc., as examples). You may want to include a map, a lapel badge and other literature such as your most recent press releases too. As you'll probably want to know who is coming and not coming, it is a good idea to ask them to confirm their intentions; a part-completed and stamped postcard for them to sign and return or a fax-back form can be helpful here. Be prepared to chase (in the nicest possible way) anyone who doesn't respond – it's a good reason for a call.

Speaking in public

The chances are that you're expected not only to set up a press conference but also to participate in it in some way; probably as a speaker, a demonstator or as an all-purpose co-ordinator. Even if you're not scheduled to speak at all, it's still wise to be well-prepared – it's not unknown for a speaker to arrive late (or not at all); and for the organizer to have to step in at the last moment to keep things going. You need to know what to say, how to say it, and how to use equipment that enables you to put over your message properly.

What to say

If you're making an introductory speech, you'll probably want to welcome speakers and the audience, and thank them for coming. Then you might introduce each speaker in turn, and say what they're going to do and cover. Logically, you'll introduce them in the order that they'll address the audience. It is also sensible to point out if or when there will be a break, that paper and pens/pencils are available and that individual speakers will be around at the end for discussion. Say that food and drinks will be provided (and when) and that press releases/press packs/samples (as appropriate) will be given out before the audience leaves.

For a speech about your business, products and services, always announce what you're going to talk about and for how long – people in the audience are thinking this, so tell them! In terms of content you'll know what you want to say. Tear up your notes; and throw them away! Let's start again – and tell them what they want to know. That is 'what's in it for me? What's this speaker going to say that will interest my readers; and make it easy for me to write a feature for them?' Tell them that and keep it short – anyone who has ever sat through a lengthy speech will tell you that's the key trick of the trade. Get on with it; say what you have to say – and shut up.

A successful demonstration means being able to describe the product, point out its key features and benefits and operate it smoothly and with good humour – all at the same time! The secret of success is to do it in advance as many times as it takes to get it right. Have you heard that saying about being able to do something so well that you can do it with your eyes shut? Try it; see if you can. It's a useful test of your ability. Remember – there's nothing worse than a blundering demonstrator who catches their thumb, has to ask for help, and covers their embarrassment with a feeble joke. So practise; again and again until you get it right.

To manage a question-and-answer session, you'll probably want to re-introduce the main speakers to the audience, highlighting their particular areas of expertise (production, sales, and so on). Pause – and then throw the session open to the floor. You'll need to indicate who should speak in turn; otherwise the session may degenerate into a free-for-all. Be ready with the answers yourself if the panel of experts stumble; a hard task (perhaps impossible), but it's your job to work out the likely questions and identify the answers in advance if you're running the show. If questions can't be answered there and then, it is essential that you promise to find out and come back to the journalist – it makes all the difference between gaining and losing publicity.

A closing speech should involve thanking speakers and the audience for attending the press conference. Try to look at as many people as you can as you do this – it implies that everyone is important and is an easy way to establish and build a rapport between you. Summarize the main point of the conference – that key message that you want to put across. Mention what happens next. Typically, refreshments are available, press packs are to be handed out and speakers are available to talk through information.

Thank everyone again; and hopefully you'll be applauded as you stand down.

You'll almost certainly have to make small talk at the end of the event; with speakers, and with the audience as they drink, eat, and look through press releases and packs. The key here is to circulate and speak to as many journalists, presenters and media people as you can. You should raise two questions with each and every person; 'have you got everything you need to write your story?' and 'what else can I do to help you write it?' Make contact with everybody there; stand by the door if necessary. And be prepared to follow through. If anyone wants anything else, get it and phone, fax or e-mail it through as soon as you can.

How to say it

Do rehearse thoroughly. Practice makes perfect – or at least much better. Some people run through what they're going to say and do in their head; or in front of a mirror. Practising in your head just doesn't work – a speech always sounds great in your imagination, but is rarely successful when you come to do it properly for the first time. And if you do it in front of a mirror, you'll find yourself concentrating on just your appearance, rather than all aspects of your speech. It's wiser to talk in front of a camcorder; and then play it back. Or rehearse in front of colleagues who will offer constructive criticism. If possible, rehearse at the venue itself so that you become accustomed to it; and feel at ease there. This is what you should be assessing.

1 **Appearance**. Wear whatever best reflects the image of your company; informal and creative, smart but casual, formal attire, or whatever. Be comfortable too – a new jacket or pair of shoes may seem like a good idea if you're striving to make a positive impression; but will distract you if that jacket itches at the collar, and those shoes pinch your feet. It's often wiser to wear your older, favourite clothes.

2 **Facial expressions**. It's said that one expression says more than a hundred words; and it's true. Smile regularly – as you talk, as you answer questions; and even if you nip your finger when you are demonstrating a product. You're a nice guy! Don't equate smiling with humour though. Steer clear of jokes and any funny comments. Everyone has a different sense of humour. For example, do you laugh when you see someone stumble in the street? Some people do; others

don't. We're all different. One thing that you can be sure of is that if you make a joke at a press conference, some of the audience will laugh, others won't understand it and a few will be offended. So play it straight at all times.

3　**Voice**. Make sure you can be heard. Hold up your head, and speak with a wide open mouth. Keep your hands away – they'll obscure your comments. Vary your pace to maintain the audience's attention. A slower pace helps to emphasize the point you're making; a faster one conveys a sense of excitement and importance. Pause every so often – it takes nerve if you're an inexperienced speaker who wants to finish as quickly as possible; but it's very effective. Not least, it adds emphasis to what you're saying at the time.

4　**Eye contact**. Nervous and inexperienced speakers never look at their audience – and their speech suffers as a result. They look at notes, the ceiling; anywhere but at the people who count – the audience. Don't make this mistake – maintain eye contract to hold attention, obtain feedback and build rapport. Look at Sarah from the *Echo* and smile at her – she's going to give you a free, one page feature, isn't she? That would cost you hundreds of pounds if you were paying for advertising space. Then look at that person you don't recognize sitting next to her and smile again – you're building an instant relationship here!

5　**Body language**. Stand up; and be seen by everyone in the room, even those at the back. Too many people sit down; especially when they're answering questions. As a result, they can't always be seen or heard – and it looks downright rude too. So stand, and look calm and in control. You can do this by keeping relatively still, and making occasional, planned movements – the sweep of an arm towards a revamped range and a jabbing finger to emphasize a main benefit can be very effective. Avoid wild and excessive movements, arm waving and striding to and fro. These make you look nervous and can distract and unsettle the audience. So too will repetitive and annoying mannerisms such as jangling your car keys and tapping your feet.

6　**Notes**. The fact of the matter is that referring to notes doesn't impress an audience. It makes you seem hesitant and uncertain. You'll not be putting over a professional image. Hopefully, whatever you have to say or do will be brief enough for you to rehearse thoroughly and then (appear to) ad-lib at the event. If necessary, cut a postcard in half, write your key points in the right order on it in capitals and hold this in the palm of your hand. You'll find it a comfort if you're a first-time speaker; and a fairly unobtrusive prop on the odd occasion. Avoid full and detailed notes though – the audience will simply think that you might as well have given them your notes as a handout rather than read them out word-for-word. And they'd be absolutely right.

Using equipment

There are many visual and audio-visual aids that can be used in a press conference in order to put across your message more effectively. Consider using product displays; of your new or revised goods or product range. In their favour, these give you the opportunity to show and demonstrate; and allow the audience to see, touch and even taste what you're talking about – all of which helps to create a powerful and lasting impression. However, bear in mind the practicalities if they're too large or heavy for the venue (perhaps a factor in your venue selection process), or are too difficult or expensive to transport. Think about the alternatives in such circumstances – large photographs or posters, samples or models, as examples. In particular, balance their cost alongside their ability to recreate the real products.

Some press conference organizers use flip-charts at such an event. These are inexpensive, informal, intimate and useful for putting over detailed information to a small and friendly audience. But – and it's a really big but – they do convey a rather amateurish, low-key image. And they require some effort from the audience who will have to write the details down – and they don't want to; they'd prefer you to do it for them, and provide handouts at the end. As a general rule, don't use flip-charts, overhead projectors, blackboards, whiteboards or anything else with a 'back-to-school' feel about it. Use visual aids that match your company image – professional and successful.

Similarly, the use of slides (with or without sound) to show overseas premises, bulky goods, or whatever, has some advantages – slides can be vivid, colourful and memorable. But sometimes they are memorable for the wrong reasons – they can be fiddly to use; being shown in the wrong order, back-to-front and/or upside-down. You may stumble over your commentary, or a taped commentary may go out of synchronization. They need to be shown in a darkened room which reduces speaker-audience contact. And again, they convey a rather amateurish image of Grandpa's holiday slide show on a wet Sunday afternoon. Avoid!

Videos are increasingly popular – used to show holiday destinations offered by the company, large products in operation, the building of a new leisure complex, and so forth. They offer many benefits – sound, music, movement, action; altogether a very memorable and lasting image. And a classy, professional one as well. But be mindful of the costs of producing these to a professional standard; you'll need to bring in outside help which is time-consuming and expensive. Refer to Chapter 5. And there is a danger that the video will take over the conference and be the most lingering memory for the audience. That's fine if it summarizes your main message; not so good if it doesn't. Let's say you're showing a video of your newly built hotel. Someone suggested filming it as it was being built, and then showing this at the beginning of the video. Your main message is the splendour of the hotel, the luxury rooms, the marvellous facilities. But all the journalists remember is the builders, the dust and the debris at the start of the video show.

Handouts of some kind – usually press releases, press packs and (occasionally) samples – are a must at press conferences. They are simple to produce and inexpensive; and give (or should give) journalists all they need to write a news story or feature. And remember, that's what your audience is here for. The biggest drawback – and one that is easy to over-come – is that they can be a distraction when you're making a speech, demonstrating a product, and so on. To resolve this, hand out pads of blank sheets of paper (with your company name and logo at the top) at the start, along with (company marked) pencils and pens. Journalists can make notes using these; if they wish. Press packs and the like can then be handed out at the end whilst you're talking informally.

So how do you decide whether or not to use visual and/or audio-visual aids in your press conference? Ask yourself various questions that will help you to reach that decision. Will they enable you to put across your message more effectively? For example, a product display may have a greater impact than a verbal description. Do they save time? Remember you're dealing with busy people here; they don't want long speeches. A summary of key points in a press pack will be more agreeable than a talk about them. Do they add variety and style to the conference? As an example, a well-made video presentation adds a new dimension to the proceedings. Do they help your audience to retain a message for longer? Bear in mind this needs to be the right message though. That product display may be memorable – but perhaps it is because of that misspelt sign; 'The Grove Studios Award Wining Photographs'. It happens.

Also consider these questions. Do they take considerable time, effort and money to arrange? Display items may need to be hired, goods trans-ported and set up, press packs written and produced, videos commissioned, and so forth. Cost them out – and judge whether they add enough to warrant the expense. Are they really necessary? Sometimes equipment is used because it's there ('we've some photos left from the exhibition; let's give them that sales film we made for our customers – that'll impress them'). They don't necessarily add to or emphasize your message. Are they easy-to-use? You'll need to make certain that the product can be demonstrated properly; and that the video can be operated smoothly. It's a sensible idea to have someone on hand just to turn on video players and deal with other tasks of this nature. You'll find it hard to talk and handle equipment simultaneously.

Managing a press conference

It is sensible to stage a full rehearsal for the press conference – your role will probably be to co-ordinate everyone, supervize the activities and make last-minute suggestions and changes. At the event itself, you'll typically perform a similar role; making sure everyone arrives on time, watching the various activities unfold, and sending everyone away happy and satisfied. Here's what you will be doing.

The rehearsal

Try to have the rehearsal at the venue; replicating what will happen on the day as closely as possible. To increase the chances of a successful event, insist on all of the speakers attending and going through their paces; even that obstinate director who's convinced he can just turn up on the day and wow the audience. He can't. You need an audience – colleagues and other employees primed to ask tricky questions can be useful. Alternatively, it's you! Study the venue as a media contact. Is it comfortable? When the room is full, can you see the speakers clearly and hear them from the back? Raise the questions that the audience will ask on the day – the most awkward, cynical questions you can think of. 'Why should our readers buy that product instead of Harrisons which is cheaper?' 'Why is yours so expensive?' See how the speakers handle them.

Of course, your primary role at rehearsals is to assess all aspects of this mock conference. In particular, the speakers, what they say and how they say it. How do they handle that unexpected question, for example? Consider the topics covered, the approach to them and their order. Is that message coming across loud and clear? And in a warm and professional manner; free from jokes and so-called humorous asides? Would it be better to have a demonstration before questions are put to the speakers, perhaps? Think about the length of the event. Be honest, is that speech becoming a little boring? Was that demonstration a little rushed? Would the conference benefit from a break in the middle (so that goods can be examined prior to questions and answers)? Take account of the venue and its facilities and services. As examples, is there any noise coming from the next room? Have you been left to operate unfamiliar equipment yourself?

If you stage a rehearsal, your most overpowering thought at the end of it will be, 'thank goodness this isn't the real thing'. Fortunately, that's the purpose of a rehearsal; to identify and eliminate any problems. You'll probably find that your main areas of concern with speakers at this stage is their over-reliance on notes, a tendency to crack jokes, and to wander away from the subject. You're going to have to tell them! With regard to the topics, approach and order, you may discover that too much attention is given to features rather than benefits for the media contacts and their audiences. Talk 'benefits, benefits, benefits' – they can't be stressed enough. 'We've put together some press packs that contain all the information you need' and 'These are the benefits for your audience . . .' are useful comments. In relation to the venue, you'll often find that you're left to your own devices. So what happens when something goes wrong? Know where help can be obtained at the real event.

The big day

At the press conference itself, your first thought must be to get everyone and everything there. Check that key media contacts (especially those that haven't responded to invitations) are coming; phone, fax through maps, stress the benefits. Remember, this event has been set up for them – they're the most important people there. Ensure that all the speakers arrive – give them a phone number to call if they're being delayed, send a car if necessary, or be prepared to step in for them. If you have to, be ready to do all of their speech or demonstration – there's nothing worse than a hesitant 'he'll be along in a minute' stand-in who hands over to a hot and sweaty, 'where are we, don't worry, I'll start again' speaker half way through. Check all is well at the venue by getting there early, and taking charge.

You'll then be performing the same supervisory role that you did at rehearsals; watching speeches, demonstrations, question-and-answer sessions and so on – and being on hand to help out. It's too late to rectify mistakes as they happen; a speaker will not take kindly to a scribbled note being pushed along the desk, and the audience will rarely be impressed by the know-all organizer who pipes up with comments such as 'If I can just add something there, Arun (or whoever)'. But you may be able to provide pointers if you've scheduled a break into the proceedings. 'Arun, you'll have noticed the audience are all making lots of notes which is distracting for them. Can you mention that we've got press packs to hand out at the end . . . that saves them writing so much.'

At the end, your main concern (and that of the speakers) must be to make certain that the media contacts have everything they need to write their news and features. Each person in that audience should be spoken to by at least one speaker; the personal touch is all-important in PR activities. They should be given whatever handouts are being distributed – stand at the exit so you can check this. Every person in that audience should receive some form of follow-on contact; a call or whatever to thank them for coming, checking that they have all they need, and an offer of further assistance – an interview or whatever.

Following up

Too often, a press conference is deemed a success or a failure without any type of proper assessment taking place at all. The MD feels he made a good speech, the food and drink were varied and plentiful and the audience seemed to be happy – so it's judged a success! Or the demonstrator stumbled over the product demonstration and there appears to be a lot of press packs left over – so it's considered a failure! Both reactions – and they're surprisingly commonplace – are naive. It's far better to evaluate the event properly. The least you can do is to sit down with everyone involved and discuss everything that happened from start to finish. In particular, address these key questions:

1   **The venue**. Did you pick a good location for the conference? Was it attractive and convenient for everyone involved – especially the audience? What comments did they make about the venue? Did the facilities and services offer everything you wanted at a fair and reasonable price? Has the event come in on budget?

2   **Speakers**. Did you select the right ones? Were they a draw to media contacts? Good at speaking, capable of demonstrating effectively,

answering questions accurately and with authority, and good at small talk? Did they put across your message, and help you to achieve your goals? Is there anything that should have been done differently?

3   **The audience**. Were the people on your media contacts list there? How many attended? How many didn't? Who sent along a replacement; and what were they like? Did they ask questions? Did you have meaningful, informal conversations with them? Did they take away press releases, packs and samples, as appropriate? Do you need to follow up on anything here – it is a wise idea to contact those who did not attend; to see if you can supply releases to them, or arrange an interview instead.

4   **The beginning** of the conference. Did everyone arrive on time? Speakers? The audience? Was everything there, ready for them? Product displays? Podium, seating, refreshment facilities? Did it start on time; and in an efficient and professional manner?

5   **The middle** of the event. Did all of the activities go well? Speeches, demonstrations, question-and-answer sessions? Were they in the right order and of a suitable length? Was your key message put across? Were the activities all interesting and informative.

6   **The end** of the press conference. Were the audience able to examine any products on display? Did all the informal conversations between speakers and the audience go well? Were the food and drink provided satisfactory? Did the audience take home press releases, press packs and samples? Have you arranged for follow-up contacts? Remember, press conferences are part of your overall PR campaign.

Of course, the bottom line for assessing the effectiveness of a press conference – indeed any PR activity – is this: 'did it generate any publicity for our business, goods and services in the media?' 'And if so, how much?' As with press releases and interviews given to the press, radio and television, you'll need to monitor the subsequent copies of newspapers, magazines and other publications closely and listen and watch radio and television programmes to spot and then evaluate the coverage you have received. We'll look at this in detail in the next chapter.

5

Running your PR campaign

■   You should view your initial batch of PR activities almost as a dummy run; as an opportunity to test your schedule and ideas, to see what seems to work successfully (and less successfully) and to amend your activities before going on any further with a PR campaign. You might even decide to employ a PR agency and/or other specialists at this stage. To do all this well, you need to know something about:

■   assessing your trial run

■   monitoring responses

■   bringing in experts

■   continuing with your PR campaign

Assessing your trial run

You have to be able to step back from your preliminary PR activities and appraise them; to decide if you are putting over the right message in the most appropriate ways and through the most suitable media to your target audience. And, if so, whether you are getting the response you want; in terms of increased recognition of your business, more sales or whatever it is that you want to achieve. Here are the types of questions you should be asking yourself – and your colleagues and advisers – as these initial PR activities unfold:

The message

Are you putting over the right message? Think again about what it is that customers want to know; to read, hear about or watch. Is it a clear and straightforward message? Some customers won't be reading, hearing or watching fully; others aren't bright enough to take in several messages at once. (Believe me, it's true – so keep it simple.) Is it a positive message? Let's be upbeat about this – if we're not, nobody else will be. Is the message really for your audience; and not just a big puffed-up piece about yourself? You should be talking benefits (for the customer) rather than features (about your firm, goods and services). Is your message true? It needs to be honest and factual; it's easy to get swept away in PR talk and hyperbole – remember that you've got to live up to that message, satisfying rather than disillusioning customers. You want them to come back again and again. Your bottom-line question is 'Are we putting out one over-riding message comprising a huge (and honest) benefit for the audience?'

PR tactics

Are you putting over the right message and in the most appropriate ways? Look once more at the options available to you; those that you are using; and any that you might be excluding. Are you issuing effective press releases? You need to give journalists some news or a story that can be turned easily into hard copy. Are you giving successful interviews? Answering the interviewer's questions honestly, putting across your key points, and conveying a warm, approachable image are essential. You're probably not the best person to judge this – so ask a respected colleague! Are you organizing winning press conferences? You have to provide the media contacts that are attending with whatever it is they've come to find out. Again, your all-important question here is this, 'Are we giving the media what they want, so that they are encouraged to pass on our message to our mutual audiences?'

Media

Are you putting across the right message in the most appropriate ways and through suitable media? Re-consider the media that you're using; or not using, as the case may be. Are the press passing on the message that you intended? You'll soon discover that some journalists will quote you accurately word-for-word; whilst others misquote you and omit key information. (Or perhaps you've already minimized the risk of this by handing out information sheets with ready-made quotes and quotable details.) Do radio and television programmes allow you to give your message to your audience as you want? You'll find that some presenters will ask you unexpected questions that distract you from what you meant to say; and that you'll miss out something. (Again, maybe you've avoided this by taking in a crib sheet to ensure you cover everything.) And your key question now is this, 'Is a complete and accurate message getting through?'

Audience

Are you putting across the right PR message in the most appropriate ways through suitable media and to your target audience? It is sensible to double-check now that the chosen media actually reach your audience. Are the newspapers, magazines and other publications that you're targeting being read by your customer base? You need to check profile and penetration facts and figures. Similarly, do the television and radio audiences match your customer base as closely as possible? Once more, there is a bottom-line question to consider, 'Are we really reaching our precise audience?'

Other considerations

Of course, there are some other aspects of your PR activities to take into account during a trial run. Look through that schedule again. Are PR activities taking place at the best times? For example, a typical problem that often occurs during a trial run is that a firm obtains publicity about a new product in the media, receives plenty of follow-up calls from customers, but has insufficient stocks available to satisfy immediate demand. It got its timings wrong! What about the frequency and duration of PR activities? You need to ensure that you are approaching the media enough times to generate interest, but are not bombarding them to the point where indifference (or annoyance) sets in. Are your PR activities well timed for media deadlines? As an example, a common problem that often arises with new PR planners is that the message, tactics and media are all 'right'; but that the timing is 'wrong'; with releases arriving just after the copy deadline. Do remember to check. What about the costs? You need to make sure that budgeted and actual costs match as closely as possible; press conferences in particular are notorious for going over budget. Your final, all-important question when assessing the trial run is this, 'Are we happy with all aspects of our PR schedule?'

Monitoring responses

The whole purpose of your PR activities is to generate publicity in the media in order to change your customers' opinion of your firm, increase sales, or whatever. You know what it is you want to achieve! So, you'll also wish to monitor the responses that you are getting to your various activities – both from the media you're approaching and, equally important, from the audiences that are (hopefully) going to go out and buy more goods and services from you.

Media responses

Appraising the response of the media to your PR activities is a relatively straightforward process. You will have already assessed how well you have issued press releases (Figure 2.7), evaluated how efficiently you conducted interviews (Figure 3.1) and decided how well you organized press conferences. And you'll be keeping some records for each area of activity – in

MEDIA RESPONSES: AN ASSESSMENT		ASSESSED BY:		DATE:	
SOURCE OF COVERAGE	DATE OF COVERAGE	PLACE/TIME	SIZE/DURATION	COST OF ADVERTISING	VALUE OF PUBLICITY

Figure 5.1 Media responses: an assessment form

order to judge performance and feedback per activity. You may find it is useful to refer back at this point just to refresh your memory. Obviously, you must ensure that all activities are of the highest possible standard so that they have the potential to be as effective as they can be; and that your findings are recorded properly so that you can appraise these responses accurately. Now – having done all of that – you need to see how far these (hopefully first-class) releases, interviews and conferences translate into hard publicity in the press and on the radio and television. Let's talk money!

So a press release, an interview or a conference has generated a news item or feature in a newspaper, magazine or other publication. That's great news – but how do we quantify it and compare the effectiveness of one press release with another; a press release with a press conference, and so on? One basic method – not perfect, but a useful measure of comparison nonetheless – is to see how much coverage has been obtained, and then calculate how much that would have cost us if we had paid for an advertisement in that same space. For example, perhaps a quarter-of-a-page feature on an inside page of the trade magazine, and a check of the rate card that was obtained when the PR schedule was first planned shows that this would cost £300 if the space were purchased for advertising. With this method – which is equally applicable to radio and television programmes if you listen, watch and time, and then refer to the rate cards – you can work out how much free publicity has been generated by each activity; and translate it into comparable, monetary terms. You will find it helpful to look at the *Media responses: an assessment form* (Figure 5.1) – and can complete it in due course.

Of course, there are other qualitative factors to take account of as well as this quantitative one. Some publications will print a feature on a left page; others on the right. Which generates the best response from readers? One will include a photograph, another will not. Does it make much difference? One journalist will adopt a straightforward, factual style of reporting; someone else will be more opinionated. Which produces the biggest response? On radio and television, you may want to decide whether a mid-morning interview is better than one in the afternoon; or if a straight interview is more effective than a discussion. You'll find that most of the people that you deal with in the media – journalists, researchers and the like – will give you some ideas as to what is most successful in their particular paper, radio station and so forth. Where possible, you can then try to build these hints into your planning; trying to get interviewed on the morning show rather than the afternoon one, and so on. (But more often, of course, you're in the hands of the media – a newspaper will run your story where it wants; regardless of your opinion.) As your PR campaign progresses, you'll be able to draw some conclusions of your own, based on the responses of the audiences.

Audience responses

These responses can be hard to measure and assess with any degree of accuracy – much depends on what exactly you are trying to appraise. You may wish to evaluate the number and types of enquiry received as a result of your PR activities if you are trying to build up a customer base. Perhaps you want to measure the number and value of sales – above and beyond your normal levels – if your aim is to boost turnover. You might even have to assess changing moods and opinions – and by how much – if your PR campaign is seeking to create a different image for your business within the marketplace.

Evaluating the number and types of enquiry that derive from press, radio and/or television publicity can be a simple process. Competition entries can be sent to the local paper and forwarded to you. On radio and television interviews, callers to the station may have their names and details recorded and sent to your firm in due course. Any direct enquiries received by your firm following media publicity may be identified readily by telling telephone operators, sales agents and so on to raise the question, 'Where did you hear about our company/new product/ service?' If a broad range of PR activities is taking place at around the same time, you might be able to separate and recognize the source of enquiries by inserting some form of 'key' (that is an identifying mark) into each piece of publicity. Say you're interviewed in three publications in one week – readers of one publication who want to know more are invited to call 'Michael James', readers of another should call 'Sophie Lewis' and so on. You may be able to do something similar on radio and television interviews; suggesting customers contact varied names, addresses, departments, reference numbers and so forth; anything that enables you to distinguish one response from another.

Often, you can measure sales in the same basic manner – simply making a record of orders sent to you via the media, asking buyers the question 'where did you hear about . . .' and by noting down varied names, addresses, departments, reference numbers and the like. For example, a sales order sent to '120–122 Major Walk' signifies that the customer is responding to an interview you gave to *The Echo* on 24 September. One forwarded to '120 Major Walk' indicates that your customer read a feature

AUDIENCE RESPONSES: ASSESSED BY: DATE:
AN ASSESSMENT

COVERAGE	VALUE OF COVERAGE	NUMBER OF ENQUIRIES	'COST' PER ENQUIRY	TOTAL SALES	'COST' PER SALE

Figure 5.2 Audience responses: an assessment form

in the *Evening Star* on 28 September. Naturally, this task has to be tackled carefully and conscientiously – some responses are received almost immediately; and then interest seems to fade away. It is tempting to stop monitoring them at that point – but you'll find that a steady stream can continue for some time afterwards (typically, until the next month's issue is sold) and can add up.

In many instances when you are appraising enquiries and sales, you can make further assessments in the same way that you did for media responses. Dividing the advertising cost of the space or time obtained by the number of enquiries received as a result of it gives you a cost-per-enquiry figure that can be used for comparison purposes. Likewise, if you divide the cost of the advertising space and time by the number and value of sales generated by it, you have further figures that can be used for evaluation purposes. Clearly, you need to take account of the number of enquiries that turn into sales and the value of those sales if your assessment is to be as meaningful as possible. And remember – the higher the 'cost', the more you've got out of it! (This is probably the only time that you'll be pleased to see 'costs' higher than expected.) Reading *Audience responses: an assessment form* (Figure 5.2) can be beneficial here; you can complete it in due course.

Assessing developing moods and opinions is tricky. They cannot automatically be quantified in terms of the number of enquiries or orders received and translated into sales. You – or perhaps specialists in market research methods – may need to interview a broad and representative mix of your customer base before and after PR activities, questioning them about their knowledge of the firm, goods and services, plus their opinions at the beginning and at the end to see if and by how much their feelings and viewpoints have been affected by your PR campaign. Of course, the ultimate aim of most PR is to increase sales at some stage; so more quantifiable assessments may be made at a later date.

Bringing in experts

Most PR planners in small and medium-sized companies conduct their own PR activities – and with some considerable success – by mixing together existing in-house expertise with some help from the various individuals within the media such as journalists, presenters and their researchers and conference executives in hotels; as well as assistance from organizations such as professional and trade bodies. However, it is useful to be aware of the experts that you can call upon, and to know something about the services that they can provide during your campaign; and the ways in which they should be assessed and subsequently chosen by you, as appropriate. Now is a good time to consider bringing in a public relations agency; and other specialists.

PR agencies

If you are thinking of hiring an agency to help with or take charge of your PR activities, you initially need to decide what you want them to do for you. Some PR agencies offer a broad and diverse range of services; including client assessment, market research, media planning and scheduling, media contacting, writing press releases, arranging interviews, organizing press conferences, and campaign assessment – much the same as you have been doing! (They've just been doing it longer.) Others focus more fully on putting clients in touch with appropriate media contacts on their database; and liaising between them in order to maximize publicity opportunities. (Although they will normally offer advice on other aspects of PR activities too.) Having already assessed the key strengths and weaknesses of your own venture (Figure 1.1, page 7) and being aware of the help and assistance available to you from the media and their representative bodies – refer to the Useful Contacts section – you should be able to identify which of your activities may be in need of some professional expertise at this stage.

Next, decide on the main attributes that you want in a PR agency. You may decide that it needs to be reputable; with an ethical approach to business so that it will not handle accounts in direct competition with each other, will disclose conflicting interests, will offer impartial advice and will maintain your confidentiality. Pick an agency that belongs to the Public Relations Consultants Association; a respected trade body with a code of conduct that members need to adhere to. Previous knowledge and experience of your type of firm, goods and services, customers, competitors and marketplace could be a key requirement too, so that its team knows how to piece together a suitable campaign for you, is familiar with what succeeds in your field and has faced and overcome common problems before. You will find that some agencies specialize in certain trades (financial, recruitment, etc.), products and services (innovative items, industrial goods, etc.) and individual media (press, television, etc.). Finding out – in due course – about their years in business, key executives, past and present clients and previous and current campaigns should provide the answers here.

Creativity is one of the most important qualities; especially if the agency is writing press releases, providing quotes for you to use in interviews and is advising you on how to set up and run press conferences. Getting to know the agency's creative team – backgrounds, earlier campaigns, thoughts and current ideas – is essential, so that you can assess this quality. Compatibility is a vital and often overlooked attribute. You, your employees, agency personnel, in-house and outside tasks and activities all need to be co-ordinated, and moving in the same direction. Sharing common ground – such as being similar-sized firms operating in the same locality or sector – can be a good sign. So too is the ability to establish quickly a warm, working relationship. You also need to be sure that the agency offers value for money – essential in all circumstances, but especially if you are running a small business operating on a limited budget. Whether you negotiate a flat fee, pay invoices for their work based on hourly or daily rates, or a variable fee linked to performance and publicity generated, you'll need to ensure this is competitively priced, and affordable. Include it in your budget calculations.

Draw up a shortlist of potentially suitable agencies by contacting the Public Relations Consultants Association. See the Useful Contacts section at the back of this book for more information about this trade body. It will supply you with details of its members; as well as providing other miscellaneous data and advice about making the right choice of agency for you. Reading through the brief notes about each individual agency, pick out those that superficially appear to have at least some of the qualities that you are looking for. As an example, you might select smaller concerns that are based near to your business so that they will be more likely to have a working knowledge of and contacts in the local media. Approach each one in turn, arranging to meet an account executive – a person who is responsible for dealing with clients and acting as a go-between them and the agency – to discuss a possible commission. Ideally, you will have at least one meeting with account executives – or directors in smaller concerns – of perhaps three agencies from which you'll make a final choice. If nothing else, you will be able to pick the brains of three experts; and can build their comments and advice into your PR campaign.

Arrange your initial meeting with an account executive on your own premises. Talk about your business, goods and services so that ideas can be formulated and suggestions made by that executive. Discuss and hand over accompanying notes and records – perhaps based on those earlier notes that you drew up. Be as open and as detailed as you feel you can be so that the agency has the raw materials needed to develop proposals that are relevant to your particular circumstances. Similarly, work through what you have discovered about your customers, competitors and the marketplace. Back up your comments with supplementary notes and supporting evidence, such as any ready-reference forms that you filled in. If you have conducted a trial run, discuss your message, tactics, the media used and so forth; and your findings to date. Show the executives around your site, let them examine your goods, talk to employees and customers – even go out and visit the competition; anything that fills in gaps in their knowledge.

Naturally, you will also want to discover more about the agency so that you can decide if it possesses the key features that you are seeking; and that its employees are able to carry out the required work on your behalf. During your meeting, try to bring these questions into the conversation: How long have you been trading? When did you join your professional body? Do you act on behalf of any of my competitors? Will you have conflicting interests by working with me? How is your agency structured? Who are your directors – and what are their backgrounds and areas of expertise? How many people work for the agency? What are their career histories; and what do each of them now do? Who do you represent – and have represented – in my trade or industry? What campaigns are you – and have been – working on? Can I see examples of your current and/or recent work? Can I have the names and contact details of your other clients? What are your terms and conditions of work? Clearly, these need to be phrased in a diplomatic manner; and at an appropriate time.

Go through all of the work that you want the agency to carry out for you – whether introducing you to their contacts, full campaign planning; or something in-between. It is essential that both parties are wholly familiar with what is wanted and required in order to avoid overlapping activities, confusion and possible ill-feeling later on. Providing written confirmation of verbal requests, offering mutual assistance without interference, sharing up-to-date information on developments, changes and problems, delivering work and paying bills on time are likely to be mutually agreeable requirements for working together well. Ask executives of favoured agencies if they would like to prepare outline proposals for presentation and analysis at a second meeting; and whether you may obtain references from your choice of its present and past clients. Other agencies need to be thanked for their time; and rejected in a gracious manner.

Second meetings with the account executives or directors of your first and second choice agencies should be held at their offices so that you can assess them further in their own environment. Ask to be shown around the premises so that you can appraise the overall property and equipment, see the interaction of staff and watch the comings and goings. Hopefully, the agency will be steadily busy, with an air of controlled chaos. Talk to the agency's employees; particularly those who are going to be responsible for planning your PR activities. Wanting to know more about them, you should raise questions such as, 'What is your role?' 'What is your background?' 'What are you working on at the moment?' 'How is that progressing?' 'Why have you chosen to draft this PR schedule?' 'What made you think of these ideas?' 'What have you worked on previously in my field?' 'What are the do's and don'ts of PR activities in my particular area?' 'What suggestions do you have for my PR campaign?' The answers to these questions – which will, of course, need to be timed carefully and phrased diplomatically – should give you a further insight into the team.

Your visit should then conclude with a brief presentation by agency personnel; setting out their thoughts and proposals for your activities. Typically, they will go through each stage of their suggested activities; in particular, the media that should be used, and the timing, frequency and duration of the campaign. Contemplate and respond to their comments, appraising whether their plans are original and viable and show a true understanding of your business circumstances. If possible, take away a written copy of their ideas for quiet consideration. Before making your final choice, do take up references from amongst their client base. Telephone rather than write in order to obtain off-the-record comments. Ask these two simple questions; 'What do you think of the such-and-such agency?' and 'Have you had any problems with them – if so, what were they?' Now make your decision.

Other specialists

If you prefer not to work with a PR agency – and there is nothing that they do that you cannot, given time and hard-earned experience – you may instead decide to go it alone, perhaps referring occasionally to numerous other experts either now or at appropriate times during your subsequent campaign. A market research company might collect additional data about your customers, rivals and the marketplace. An illustrator could design attractive artwork for you; company letterheads, logos, a house style for your stationery and posters for your press conferences. A photographer can produce photos to accompany press releases, to be used in brochures, catalogues or press packs, or blown up for display purposes at press conferences. A copywriter can help you to draft exciting and informative text; whilst a typesetter can show you distinctive typefaces to choose from. All of these specialists can help to make your PR activities more successful.

Consider which experts may be of value and of active assistance to you. Gaps in your knowledge about your diverse and widespread customer base could prove damaging. For example, being unaware of customers' readership habits may mean that you target the wrong newspapers and magazines for publicity purposes. The MD's enthusiasm for amateur photography can cause problems. The difference between an enlarged amateur photograph and a professionally taken one is striking; especially when it's a metre square and being looked at by a cynical reporter attending your first press conference. Relying on your computer program to show you a range of logos and typefaces for your stationery can be unwise; every other small business owner and manager is doing the same. An illustrator and typesetter may offer something unique. Even if you can handle all of your PR activities in-house, it is still wise to liaise with specialists so that you can derive a broader and more complete understanding of what you need to do.

Obtain the names, addresses and brief details of market research companies from their leading trade bodies – the Association of Market Survey Organisations Limited and the Market Research Society. Lists and details of other specialists – illustrators, photographers, copywriters, typesetters – can be obtained by contacting the Association of Illustrators, the British Institute of Professional Photography, the British Printing Industries Federation and the Society of Typographic Designers. This way, you know that members have – in most cases – reached certain professional standards, and abide by a code of conduct and standards. More information and personal recommendations (always the best way to pick an expert) may be forthcoming from well-informed business colleagues and associates; enabling you to shortlist perhaps three or four of each that are worth talking to. See the Useful Contacts section at the back of this book for details of these professional bodies.

Your dealings with market research companies, illustrators and the like will probably progress in much the same way that they will with PR agencies. You will identify the key qualities that you want them to possess – not least, a lively imagination, a working knowledge of your field, an understanding of your particular circumstances, and competitive charges. Then, you will want to get to know each of them as well as you can to see how far they match your criteria; asking gently probing questions over the telephone, meeting them in person, looking round their premises, talking to their employees, studying their work and so on.

At the same time – and one of the best ways of assessing the suitability of a specialist – see how interested they are in you; your firm, goods and services. If they are to do their job properly, they will want to find out all about you and the work that you want them to do. You will need to chat – and be questioned about – your business, goods and services, customers, rivals and the marketplace you are operating within; and your PR activities and schedule, as appropriate. (Logically, a copywriter will want to know all about everything if they are to produce relevant and consistent copy for press releases and other promotional material; whereas a typesetter might simply ask how you want your business to be perceived in the market so that a suitable choice of typefaces can be recommended.) As relevant, walk experts around your property, letting them see your products, watch services being carried out, meeting employees and so forth.

Clarify and discuss the work that you want to hand over; perhaps to ascertain what customers think of your firm, products and services, to photograph your employees performing services for satisfied customers, or to produce a banner or product display material for your press conferences. Explain precisely what you are looking for, by when and for how much money – remember your budgetary constraints. Check what they want from you – accessible staff, regular updates and no amateurish interference. Go through your ideas to see which ones can be carried out in practice. Obtain references – from two or three of their most recent clients – and take them up. A typical problem that might otherwise be encountered is that a specialist produces excellent material but doesn't deliver on time; that person is of no use to you if you're working to a tight deadline.

Continuing with your PR campaign

Mindful of your evaluation of your test PR activities, you can now set about revising your PR schedule accordingly. Make sure your message is streamlined, and is clear and simple. Decide which tactics are most effective for you – perhaps press conferences are too costly; and don't produce results above and beyond those achieved by press releases. Amend your media contacts list – maybe that local free newspaper gives you publicity; but it's time-consuming to arrange, and does not appear to produce any benefits for you. Consider dropping it, at least for the time being. Think about targeting different groups of customers at different times; now that you've got this experience behind you. And amend your schedule – possibly having learned the hard way that some media do not use material delivered on the copy deadline day, however professional and well-written it may be.

It is imperative that you continue with your PR campaign on a step-by-step basis, perhaps carrying out one month's activities at a time before assessing them again. Always be conscious of the fact that your early opinions are incomplete; they may be inaccurate too. You may have deduced this, that and the other – but never forget that you are working with limited data; and are still inexperienced at this stage. Don't be in too much of a hurry to publicize yourself until you have gained a more substantial body of evidence and have filled in any gaps in your knowledge.

Also, internal and external factors will change and develop as time goes by. Internally, your firm may consolidate, grow and diversify, acquiring different strengths and weaknesses. Products and services may come and go. So too may rivals – a publication that rarely gave you publicity might be more welcoming, now that one of its main advertisers has closed down. Political, social and other influences might affect the marketplace – and these can all have knock-on effects on your activities and campaign. To be the most successful PR planner, you must adopt a hands-on approach; constantly analysing your activities and the results over and over again; and never being afraid to make changes as necessary; even to long held-practices. Read The PR Planner's Checklist (Figure 5.3) at this point; and regularly from now on as you run your successful PR campaigns.

THE PR PLANNER'S CHECKLIST

PLANNING PR ACTIVITIES

- Have you assessed your business, products and services, competitors and the marketplace?
- Are you aware of the benefits and drawbacks of using press releases, interviews and/or press conferences as your PR tactics?
- Do you know all about newspapers, magazines, other publications, the radio and television; their characteristics, strengths and weaknesses as PR media?
- Do you have a mind's-eye view of your typical customer; and know all about their habits too?
- Have you got one overriding message to put across to your audience using the right tactics and media; and all at the best times?

ISSUING PRESS RELEASES

- Do you have an extensive and useful press list?
- Are you aware of what you want to say in your press releases?
- Have you chosen effective paper, colour and typefaces?
- Do your layout, contents and English re-inforce rather than detract from your message?
- Do your photographs, captions and any accompanying material help rather than hinder your press releases?
- Are you familiar with the pros and cons of circulating press releases by post, fax and/or e-mail; and the do's and don'ts for success?
- Are you ready and able to handle responses to your press releases?
- Do you know how to monitor replies and keep records of your press release activities?

MANAGING INTERVIEWS

- Are you conscious of the do's and don'ts of interviewing success?

Figure 5.3 The PR Planner's Checklist

- Do you recognize the key characteristics of press interviews; and know how to handle them effectively?
- Have you full understanding of the main feature of radio interviews; and the knowledge needed to be a successful interviewee?
- Do you know the particular characteristics of television interviews; and how to manage them well?
- Are you prepared and capable of handling a crisis; and unexpected approaches from the media?
- Are you familiar with what to do after interviews; to achieve PR success?

ORGANIZING PRESS CONFERENCES
- Do you recognize the 'who-what-when-where-why' framework for planning a press conference; and know how to apply it?
- Are you able to pick the right venue for a particular occasion; and the most appropriate speakers and invited audience as well?
- Can you speak effectively in public; knowing what to say, how to say it, and using equipment efficiently too?
- Are you ready to manage a press conference; both in rehearsal and on the day itself?
- Do you know which questions to ask to follow up the event; and assess its success?

RUNNING YOUR PR CAMPAIGN
- Do you evaluate trial activities carefully – in particular, the message, tactics, media and the target audience?
- Can you monitor the responses to your PR activities; both from the media and the audience?
- Do you recognize the value of bringing in experts such as PR agencies; and know how to make the right choice?
- Are you a successful PR planner; ready to continue with your campaign?

Figure 5.3 The PR Planners Checklist (continued)

Useful Contacts

Advertising Association
Abford House
15 Wilton Road
London SW1V 1NJ
0171 828 2771

Association of British Chambers of Commerce
Manning House
22 Carlisle Place
London SW1P 1JA
0171 565 2000

Association of Conference Executives
Riverside House
High Street
Huntingdon
Cambridgeshire PE18 6SG
01480 475595

Association of Illustrators
32–38 Saffron Hill
London EC1N 8FH
0171 831 7377

Association of Independent Radio Companies Limited
Radio House
46 Westbourne Grove
London W2 5SH
0171 727 2646

Association of Market Survey Organisations Limited
16 Creighton Avenue
London N10 1NU
0181 444 3692

Audit Bureau of Circulation Limited
Black Prince Yard
207 High Street
Berkhamsted
Hertfordshire HP4 1AD
01442 870800

BBC
Broadcasting House
London W1A 1AA
0181 743 8000

British Association of Conference Towns
Elizabeth House
22 Suffolk Street
Queensway
Birmingham B1 1LS
0121 616 1400

British Institute of Professional Photography
2 Amwell End
Ware
Hertfordshire SG1 2HN
01920 464011

British Printing Industries Federation
11 Bedford Row
London WC1R 4DX
0171 242 6904

Broadcasting Standards Commission
7 The Sanctuary
London SW1P 3JS
0171 233 0544

Bulk Verified Services
Black Prince Yard
207 High Street
Berkhamsted
Hertfordshire HP4 1AD
01442 870800

CBD Research Limited
15 Wickham Road
Beckenham
Kent BR3 2JS
0181 650 7745

Central Statistical Office
Great George Street
London SW1P 3AQ
0171 270 3000

Independent Radio Sales
163 Eversholt Street
London NW1 1BU
0171 388 8787

Independent Television Commission
33 Foley Street
London W1P 7LB
0171 255 3000

Institute of Practitioners in Advertising
44 Belgrave Square
London SW1X 8QS
0171 235 7020

Institute of Public Relations
The Old Trading House
15 Northburgh Street
London EC1V 0PR
0171 253 5151

Joint Industry Committee for National Readership Surveys
44 Belgrave Square
London SW1X 8QS
0171 235 7020

London Business School
Sussex Place
Regents Park
London NW1 4SA
0171 265 5050

Maclean Hunter Limited
33–39 Bowling Green Lane
London EC1R 0DA
0171 508 8000

Market Research Society
15 Northburgh Street
London EC1V 0AH
0171 490 4911

Meetings Industry Association
34 High Street
Broadway
Worcestershire WR12 7DT
01386 858572

Newspaper Publishers Association
34 Southwark Bridge Road
London SE1 9EU
0171 928 6928

Newspaper Society
Bloomsbury House
Bloomsbury Square
74–77 Great Russell Street
London WC1B 3DA
0171 636 7014

Periodical Publishers Association
Queen's House
28 Kingsway
London WC2B 6JR
0171 404 4166

Public Relations Consultants Association
Willow House
Willow Place
Victoria
London SW1P 1JH
0171 233 6026

Radio Authority
Holbrook House
14 Great Queen Street
London WC2B 5DG
0171 430 2724

Radio Joint Audience Research
44 Belgrave Square
London SW1X 8QS
0171 235 7020

Society of Typographic Designers
21–27 Seagrove Road
London SW6 1RP
0171 381 4258

Verified Free Distribution Limited
Black Prince Yard
207 High Street
Berkhamsted
Hertfordshire HP4 1AD
01442 870800

Further reading

Books

How to Organise a Conference by Iain Maitland (1996). Published by Gower Publishing Group, Gower House, Croft Road, Aldershot, Hampshire GU11 3HR. Tel: 01252 331551.

A detailed, practical guide to staging a conference; aimed at managers and executives who are managing such an event for the first time; and who need to acquire skills and expertise quickly. Price on application.

The Small Business Advertising Handbook by Iain Maitland (1998). Published by Cassell plc, 125 Strand, London WC2R 0BB. Tel: 0171 420 5555.

A 500-page, in-depth guide to advertising in the press, on radio and via direct mail and exhibitions; step-by-step advice, helpful checklists and practical examples. Price on application.

Magazines

Campaign published by Haymarket Marketing Publications Limited, 174 Hammersmith Road, London W6 7JP. Tel: 0171 413 4570.

A weekly magazine full of news and information about the media. Well worth a look. Current cover price and subscription rates on application.

Creative Review published by Centaur Communications Limited, St Giles House, 50 Poland Street, London W1V 4AX. Tel: 0171 439 4222.

A monthly magazine full of fascinating features and advice on creative marketing issues. Latest cover price and subscription rates on application.

PR Week published by Haymarket Marketing Publications Limited, 174 Hammersmith Road, London W6 7JP. Tel: 0171 413 4520.

A weekly magazine containing news and features on public relations issues. A 'must-read' publication for all PR planners. Present cover price and subscription rates on application.

Directories

British Conference Destinations Directory published by the British Association of Conference Towns, Elizabeth House, 22 Suffolk Street, Queensway, Birmingham, B1 1LS. Tel: 0121 616 1400.

A free annual guide to conference destinations throughout the British Isles. The entry for each town or city includes details of conference facilities, contact names and other data. A useful signpost for PR planners looking to run press conferences away from their own premises.

British Rate and Data (BRAD) published by Maclean Hunter Limited, 33–39 Bowling Green Lane, London EC1R 0DA. Tel: 0171 508 8000.

Huge, 600–page directory providing in-depth data about key media within the United Kingdom. Essential reading; but in your local, larger library where it can be studied without charge.

Conference Green and Blue Books published by Benn Business Information Services, PO Box 20, Sovereign Way, Tonbridge, Kent TN9 1RQ. Tel: 01732 362666.

Known as the bibles of the conference industry, the *Green Book* lists conference venues, unusual locations etc; and the *Blue Book* details technical information regarding venue capacity, dimensions, etc. Helpful reading – current prices on application.

Directory of British Trade Associations published by CBD Research, 15 Wickham Road, Beckenham, Kent BR3 2JS. Tel: 0181 650 7745.

An annual directory listing and detailing professional and trade associations in Britain. Refer to it in your nearest, larger library.

Glossary of terms

ABC certificate. An 'Audit Bureau of Circulation' Certificate providing independent verification of the number of copies of a publication distributed or sold.

Account executive. A person employed by an advertising or PR agency to work on clients' behalf.

Advance booking discount. A price reduction on advertising packages booked some time ahead.

Appropriation. A sum of money set aside for certain activities. Better known as a budget.

Bleed off. The extension of text and/or illustrations to the edge of a page.

BVS certificate. A 'Bulk Verified Services' Certificate supplying independent verification of the average number of copies of a free publication distributed in bulk.

Camera-ready copy. Final text and illustrations ready for photographing and printing.

Circulation. The number of copies of an issue of a publication sold, delivered or handed out.

Classified advertisement. A line-by-line advertisement under a general heading such as 'For Sale'.

Combined discount. A price reduction on offer when advertisements are transmitted over more than one area.

Consumer-specific title. A magazine for special interest groups, such as sci-fi enthusiasts.

Contract discount. A price reduction available to advertisers who spend more than a certain amount of money over a set period of time. Also referred to as an 'expenditure discount' and a 'volume discount'.

Controlled circulation. A method of circulation whereby a publication is made available to a limited number of named businesses and/or individuals only.

Copy. A name given to text (or text and illustrations) that is going to be published.

Copy deadline. Date and time by which copy must be submitted for publication.

Cost per thousand. The cost of reaching every 1,000 people via a particular medium.

Display advertisement. A bordered advertisement.

Double-page spread. Two, side-by-side pages. Also called a 'DPS'.

Ear. The space(s) to the side(s) of the front page title. Otherwise known as an 'ear piece'.

Facing matter. The material facing a particular position in a publication. Also called 'FM'.

Fixing charge. A surcharge on advertisements transmitted at certain, more popular times.

Gatefold. A sheet with folded-in leaves.

General consumer magazine. A publication of interest to many types of people.

Insert. An item inserted into a publication; either loose or bound-in.

Island position. An advertising position surrounded by editorial matter.

Key. An identifying element specific to particular coverage that enables the response to it to be identified.

Linage. The cost per line of a classified advertisement. Also called 'line rate'.

Marketing guide. An information pack for prospective advertisers; of equal use to PR planners. Sometimes known as a 'media' guide' or 'media pack'.

Mono. Black and white production.

Next matter. The material next to a particular position in a publication. Also referred to as 'NM'.

Package. A group of advertising spots purchased by an advertiser.

Pass-on readership. The total number of people who look at a copy of a publication.

Penetration. The extent to which a media audience reaches the target audience.

Profile. The make-up of an audience; by age, sex, social grade etc.

Proofs. Copies of material produced for checking prior to amendments and production of the finished version.

Rate card. A sheet or pamphlet providing advertising and other data about a particular medium. Supplied separately or as part of a marketing guide.

Run of paper. An arrangement whereby material will be placed anywhere within a publication as the publisher's discretion. Sometimes called 'run of press' or 'ROP'.

Semi-display advertisement. A display advertisement in a classified section of a publication.

Single column centimetre. The standard unit of advertising space sold in a publication; one column wide by one centimetre deep. Often abbreviated to 'SCC'.

Single spot. The addition of one colour to text and/or illustrative material. Also called 'spot colour'.

Social grades. Ways in which the general public are classified; according to the occupation of the head of the household.

Solus position. A position whereby an advertisement is the only one on a page.

Special position. A guaranteed position; as chosen by an advertiser.

Spot. The standard unit of advertising time; typically 30 seconds' duration.

Test market discount. A price reduction offered to first-time advertisers. Sometimes known more simply as a 'first-time discount'.

Type area. The part of a page covered by text and illustrations.

Typesetter. The person responsible for setting out text and illustrations onto the printed page.

Voucher copy. A complimentary copy of a publication.

VFD certificate. A 'Verified Free Distribution' Certificate that confirms the average number of copies of a publication distributed free of charge.

Index

References in bold indicate figures.